Ukulele

English Folk Tunes

37 Traditional Pieces for Ukulele

Edited and arranged by Colin Tribe

ED 13569D
ISMN 979-0-2201-3839-3
ISBN 978-1-84761-500-8

Schott

Mainz · London · Madrid · Paris · New York · Tokyo · Beijing
© 2013 SCHOTT MUSIC Ltd, London · Printed in Germany

ED 13569D
British Library Cataloguing-in-Publication Data.
A catalogue record for this book is available from the British Library

ISMN 979-0-2201-3839-3
ISBN 978-1-84761-500-8

© 2013 Schott Music Ltd, London

All rights reserved. No part of this publication may be reproduced, stored in
a retrieval system, or transmitted, in any form or by any means, electronic, mechanical,
photocopying, recording or otherwise, without prior written permission from
Schott Music Ltd, 48 Great Marlborough Street, London W1F 7BB

French translation: Michaëla Rubi
German translation: Heike Brühl
Design and typesetting by www.adamhaystudio.com
Cover photography: thinkstockphotos.com
Music setting and page layout by Bev Wilson
Printed in Germany · S&Co. 8937

Contents

Introduction   4
Understanding the Notation   5
Example: Amazing Grace   6

The Pieces
(Page No.)

1	As I Walked Forth	7
2	Amazing Grace	8
3	Blaydon Races	10
4	Botany Bay	11
5	Blow the Wind Southerly	12
6	Early One Morning	14
7	Blow the Man Down	16
8	Dashing Away with the Smoothing Iron	17
9	English Country Garden	18
10	God Rest Ye Merry Gentleman	19
11	Greensleeves	20
12	Heart of Oak	21
13	I Gave My Love a Cherry	22
14	Johnny Todd	23
15	Married to a Mermaid	24
16	Morning Has Broken	25
17	Newcastle	26
18	O No, John	27
19	Over the Hills and Far Away	28
20	Raggle Taggle Gypsy	29
21	Sam Hall	30
22	When the Boat Comes In	31
23	Scarborough Fair	32
24	Spanish Ladies	34
25	Stewball	35
26	The British Grenadiers	36
27	The Foggy Foggy Dew	37
28	The Girl I Left Behind Me	38
29	The Lass of Richmond Hill	39
30	The Keel Row	40
31a	The Sailor's Hornpipe (In F)	41
31b	The Sailor's Hornpipe (In G)	42
32	The Water is Wide	43
33	The Lincolnshire Poacher	46
34	We Wish You a Merry Christmas	47
35	The Ploughboy	48
36	A Young Sailor Cut Down in His Prime	50
37	What Shall We Do With the Drunken Sailor?	53
	Notes on the Tunes	54
	Author biography	62
	VCM Grade Listings	63
	Track List	64

Translations/ Traduction/ Übersetzungen
French and German translations of the introductory text
are available as free pdf downloads from:
http://www.schott-music.com/englishfolkukulele/

Les traductions française et allemande du texte d'introduction peuvent être
téléchargées gratuitement au format pdf à l'adresse suivante :
http://www.schott-music.com/englishfolkukulele/

Französische und deutsche Übersetzung der Einleitung als kostenloser pdf-
Download unter: **http://www.schott-music.com/englishfolkukulele/**

Introduction

In recent years there has been a resurgence of interest in the Ukulele fuelled in part by its relative cheapness, portability and contributing social factors. The many hundreds, possibly thousands of Ukulele groups that have sprung up in the UK and worldwide provide musicians with a non-threatening platform to perform on, and only require a little strumming knowledge which can be learned in a couple of weeks.

Originating from early guitar-type instruments, the Ukulele was first developed by Portuguese immigrants to Hawaii. The Hawaiian tradition still continues with the beautiful playing of musicians such as Israel Kamakawiwo'ole (Izzy). Additionally, American and British players of the past such as Ukulele Ike, George Formby and Roy Smeck are still revered, and have been joined by a new generation of players often emerging through media outlets such as YouTube. In this vein the virtuoso work of Jake Shimabukuro has awakened many to the possibilities of the instrument.

In Canada, an established history of educational programmes are being continued by another brilliant player James Hill, and in the UK, the Victoria College of Music have an exam syllabus for the Ukulele that I wrote and is now taken by students all over the world. With this in mind it was wonderful to be invited to compile a set of arrangements of English Folk Tunes for the Schott World Music series.

Although this is not a Tutor, some of the techniques I use will be new to many Ukulele players who are perhaps taking their first tentative steps in Fingerstyle playing. As a guide, later in this introduction, I have discussed the playing techniques used in *Amazing Grace* as I have recorded it in the audio tracks. A video demonstration can be found on the Schott Music website at **www.schott-music.com/englishfolkukulele**. Tips on playing the other tunes in the book can be found in the **Notes on the Tunes** section together with a short description of each piece's historical background.

As both folk music in general, and the Ukulele tradition in particular both belong to worlds that rely on individual interpretation rather than Musical Pedagogy, any techniques and styles you bring to playing can be seen as valid and enriching. It is also in the nature of this music that repetitions often occur within pieces, and so it is for players to explore and find new ways to make the music varied and interesting.

As most of the pieces are also songs, lyrics for the opening verse that go with each tune are included and you can find full versions on the Schott website at **www.schott-music.com/englishfolkukulele**.

My thanks go to Wendy Lampa at Schott Music, London for joining in the move to recognise and raise the status of the ukulele, my son Rob Tribe for recording three of the tracks on electric ukulele and my son-in-law Jeremy Goldsmith for conducting historical research.
The audio tracks were performed on a variety of LEHO ukuleles. Demo performances of several of the tunes in this collection can also be seen on my Youtube channel (**www.youtube.com/user/colinrtribe**) with more to be added in the future. Currently, those pieces included are: *Early One Morning, English Country Garden, I Gave My Love A Cherry, Morning has Broken, Scarborough Fair, The Water is Wide.*

Colin Tribe
March 2013

Audio files can be downloaded for free with the following voucher code on **www.schott-music.com/online-material**: **vj7r9y4H**

Audio-Dateien können unter **www.schott-music.com/online-material** mit diesem Gutscheincode umsonst heruntergeladen werden: **vj7r9y4H**

Understanding the Notation

To simplify the reading of the music and show fretting I have included tablature staves for each tune; a standard practice nowadays. The tuning uses a re-entrant system where the strings are **not** in pitch order from bottom to top as on the violin, guitar, mandolin etc. The fourth string is in fact an octave higher than you would expect, although some players do use a Low G tuning as it is called. Players in Canada and Norway frequently use a D tuning (A D F# B); this would sound a tone higher than that which is notated.

The right hand fingers are assigned letters as for Classical Guitar:

p(ulgar)=thumb, *i*(ndice)=index, *m*(edio)=middle, *a*(nular)=ring finger

Although they are often positioned with *p* on 4, *i* on 3, *m* on 2, *i* on 1, repeated playing of the same string is often better with an alternating *i,m,i,m*.

Digital chords – I use a 4 digit number system, corresponding to the tablature fret numbers, in **bold type** so for instance A minor can be shown in these three ways – as a chord diagram, staff notation & tablature and written as **2000**.

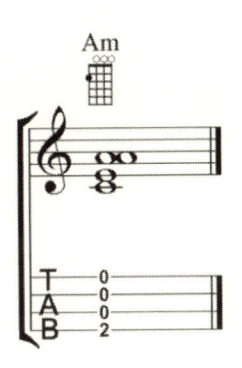

If frets above 9 are referred to in the text, then I've added a comma between them. An X indicates that you should not sound that string.

Individual notes will be written as numbers for the string and indices for the fret so 1^2 will mean first string, second fret.

Left Hand fingers are shown as numbers 1,2,3,4.

A Barre is a fingering where one finger presses several strings simultaneously at a particular fret.

Chord Symbols are shown for each piece.

Here is a full notation and tablature chart (below) to help you locate notes on the ukulele fret board and help you find alternative fingerings if mine include stretches too uncomfortable for you.

Example: Amazing Grace

All the arrangements are in two voices. Voice 1, which has stems pointing upwards, is the melody. Voice 2 is an accompanying part and has downward pointing stems. Whilst the melody is the fixed part of the arrangements, the accompaniment gives a lot of room for your interpretation. You could simplify the whole arrangement and just play one accompanying chord for each bar (after the introduction) like this -

A good way to learn each piece is to first learn the melody and then do it as shown above to get the feel of the chord shapes you will be using for the accompaniment. All references from now on are to the score on pages 8–9

Bar 1 of *Amazing Grace* begins with a tricky *pim* roll on strings 321 which gives a fast arpeggio effect and is more stressed than the pinched pim that I use on the next two chords in the bar. Again, it is individual interpretation that is important and if you have not developed that roll smoothly yet, just pinch or strum a bit more strongly when on beat 1 – anything that helps to enforce the rhythmic 3 beat feel of the bar – rather like an "oom-pah-pah".

Bar 2 begins with the full *pima* roll before then the first melody notes are played with *m,a*, followed by another *pima* roll in Bar 3. Stressing the last note of this arpeggio (the top string played with *a*) slightly to bring out the melody note A is a very effective technique but can take a while to master. The notes of the chord are held with the left hand whilst the right hand continues with the melody on string 1. In Bar 3 the accompaniment on beat 2 is played with a light brush stroke with either *i* or *im* or *ima*. Don't worry about re-hitting the top string A, this kind of recycling of notes is a common idea with the limited resources of the instrument and an excellent way to increase the sense of harmonic continuation. On beat 3 I use a pinch stroke with *pma* followed by *i* to give the rhythmic context, using a pull off from fret 4 to fret 2 to 0 (open) using fingers 4 and 3.

The next technique to point out is the *hammer-on* in Bar 8 which is immediately followed by a slide with the little finger to get from fret 4 to 7 smoothly whilst the 1st finger plays a barre at the 4th fret (bar 9). This chord shape is fundamental to my arrangements and is not too hard compared with the agonies that guitarists go through, although it will be apparent whether the A string is firmly pressed or not as you play the next hammer-on, on beat 3 in bar 10.

Section 1 ends with the opening figure repeated at bar 17 but from bar 19 the accompaniment uses arpeggios instead of the brushed chords. Here it is best to use *pimi*, with variations for the last beat of the bar depending on the melodic content. Be careful with Bar 33, and use *im* on beat 2 and *pi* on beat 3 before the final *pima* roll in the last bar where I have included a higher C♯ in the final chord.

A few final points

The chord symbols above the music refer to the chord of choice for a second player and not necessarily to the chord shown in the arrangement itself. For instance the E7 in bar 9 would need the chord **4247** rather than **4447** as shown, but that is hard to accomplish and makes the hammer-on effect in bar 10 really tough. Therefore, in arranging I have made compromises that hopefully make the piece playable as well as retaining the essential musical ingredients.

If using the arrangement with a singer then you may need to modify the number of verses played. Strive for variety in the accompanying figures so that verses have variation. These can start from the arrangements in the book, for instance a pattern for *Amazing Grace* might start:

Verse 1 One chord per bar

Verse 2 Light brush strokes in the pattern

Verse 3 Arpeggios

Verse 4 Strumming 3 to the bar

You could add in a solo instrumental verse as well, or use the book arrangement to add the melody behind the singer. Often the second verse in the recordings is played quite freely with more strumming included.

Check that the chosen Key is suitable for the singer and transpose the chords if necessary.

1. As I Walked Forth

Trad. arr. Colin Tribe

2. Amazing Grace

Trad. arr. Colin Tribe

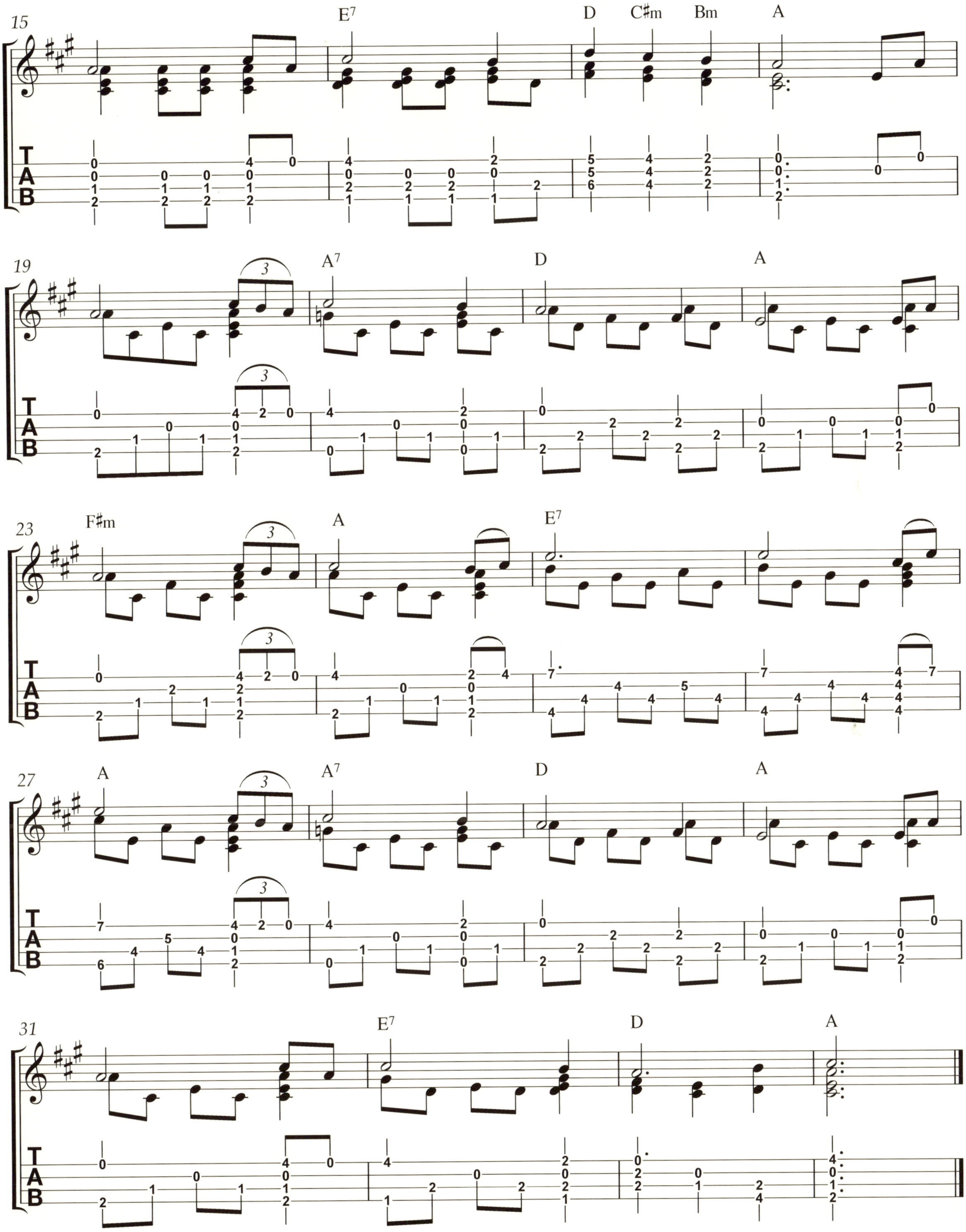
15
E7
D C♯m Bm
A
19
A7
D
A
23
F♯m
A
E7
27
A
A7
D
A
31
E7
D
A

3. Blaydon Races

Trad. arr. Colin Tribe

4. Botany Bay

Trad. arr. Colin Tribe

5. Blow the Wind Southerly

Trad. arr. Colin Tribe

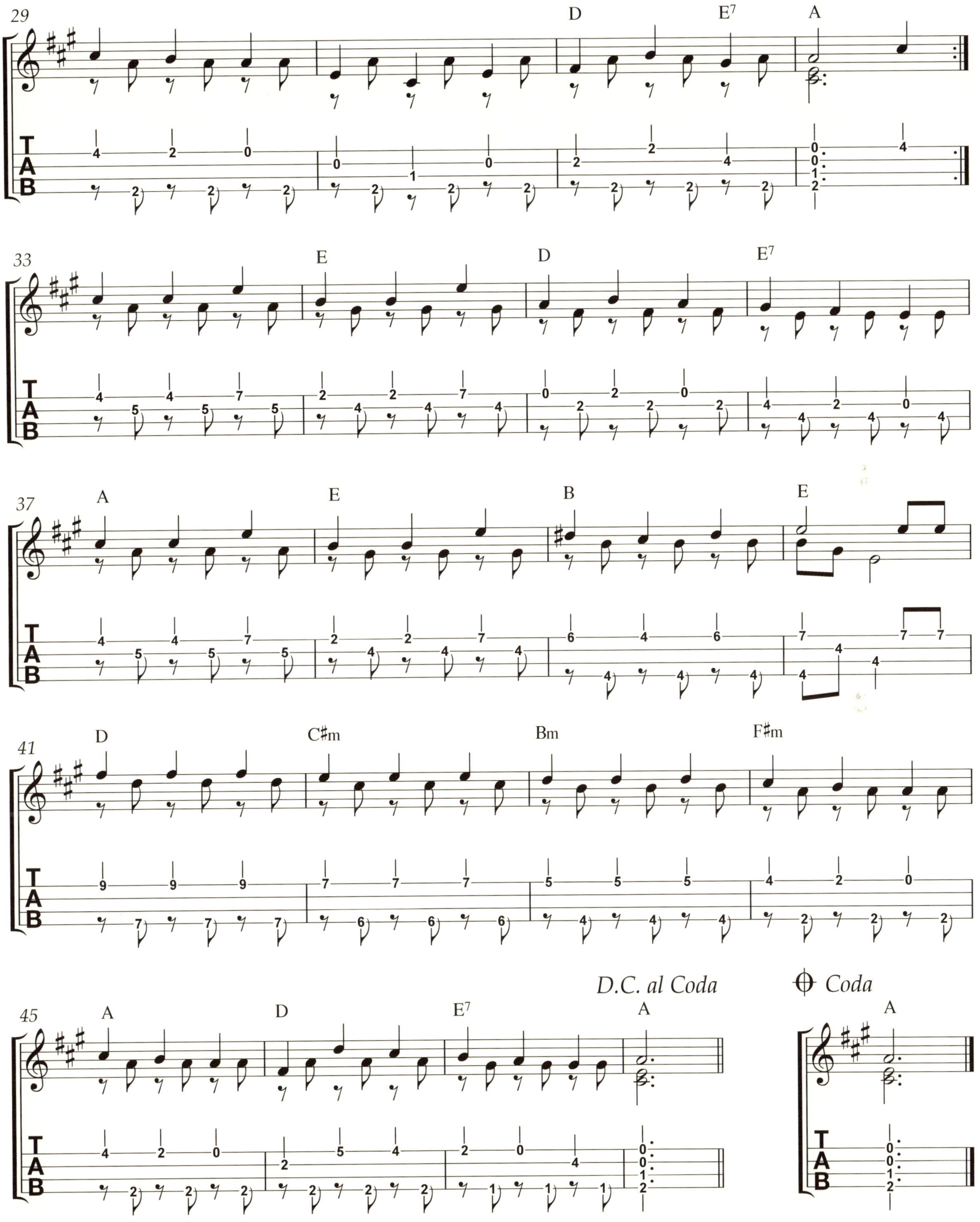
29
D
E7
A
33
E
D
E7
37
A
E
B
E
41
D
C♯m
Bm
F♯m
45
A
D
E7
D.C. al Coda
A
Coda
A

6. Early One Morning

Trad. arr. Colin Tribe

15

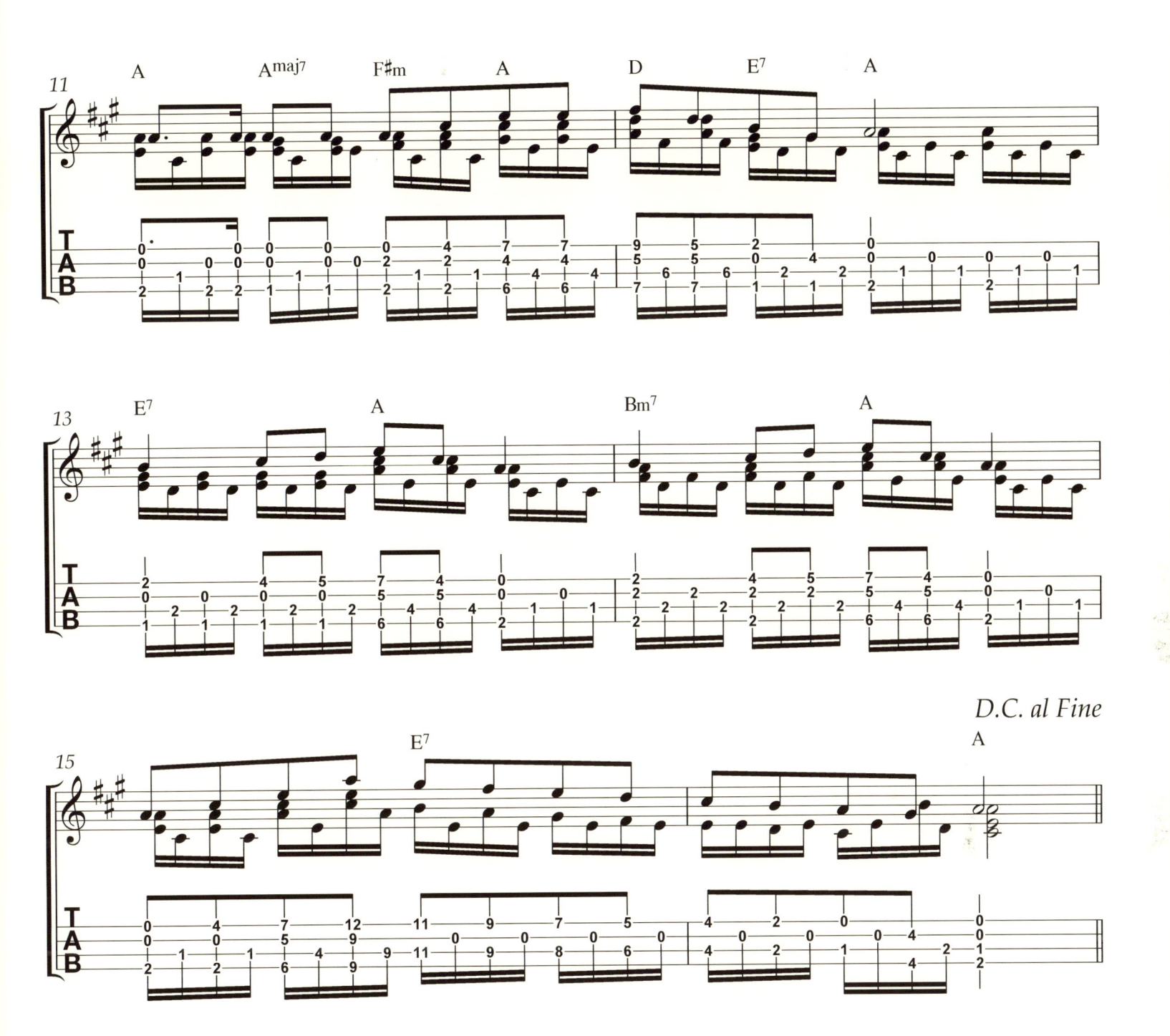

7. Blow the Man Down

Trad. arr. Colin Tribe

8. Dashing Away with the Smoothing Iron

Trad. arr. Colin Tribe

9. English Country Garden

Trad. arr. Colin Tribe

10. God Rest Ye Merry Gentlemen

Trad. arr. Colin Tribe

© 2013 Schott Music Ltd, London

11. Greensleeves

Trad. arr. Colin Tribe

© 2013 Schott Music Ltd, London

12. Heart of Oak

Trad. arr. Colin Tribe

13. I Gave My Love a Cherry
(The Riddle Song)

Trad. arr. Colin Tribe

© 2013 Schott Music Ltd, London

14. Johnny Todd

Trad. arr. Colin Tribe

Track 15

15. Married to a Mermaid

Trad. arr. Colin Tribe

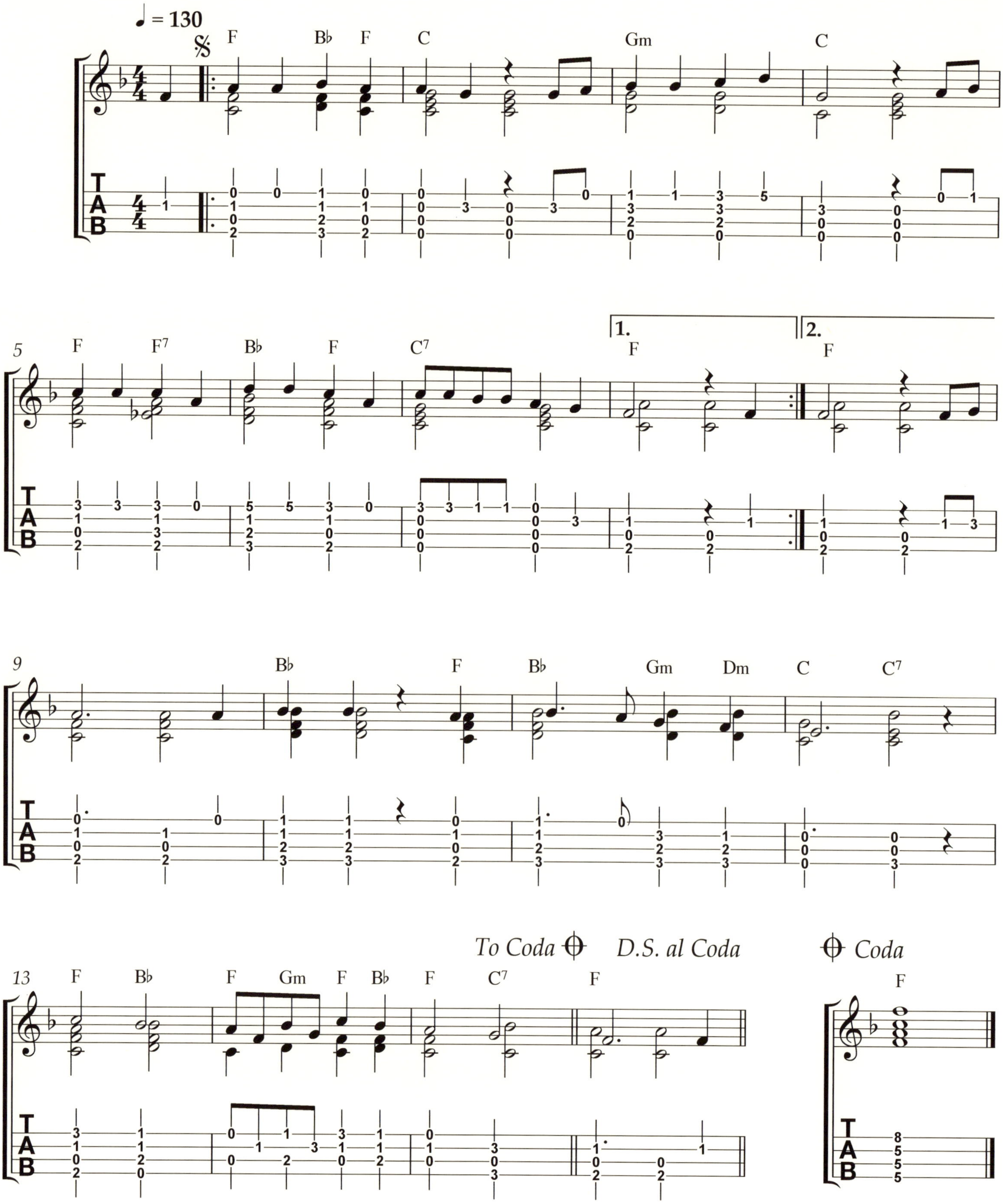

16. Morning Has Broken

Trad. arr. Colin Tribe

17. Newcastle

Trad. arr. Colin Tribe

18. O No, John

Trad. arr. Colin Tribe

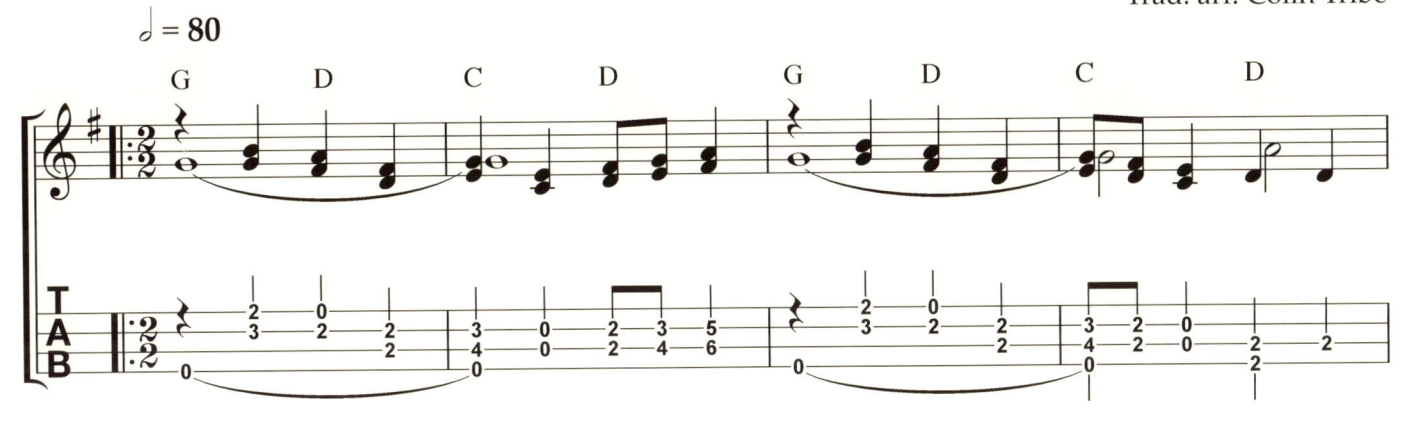

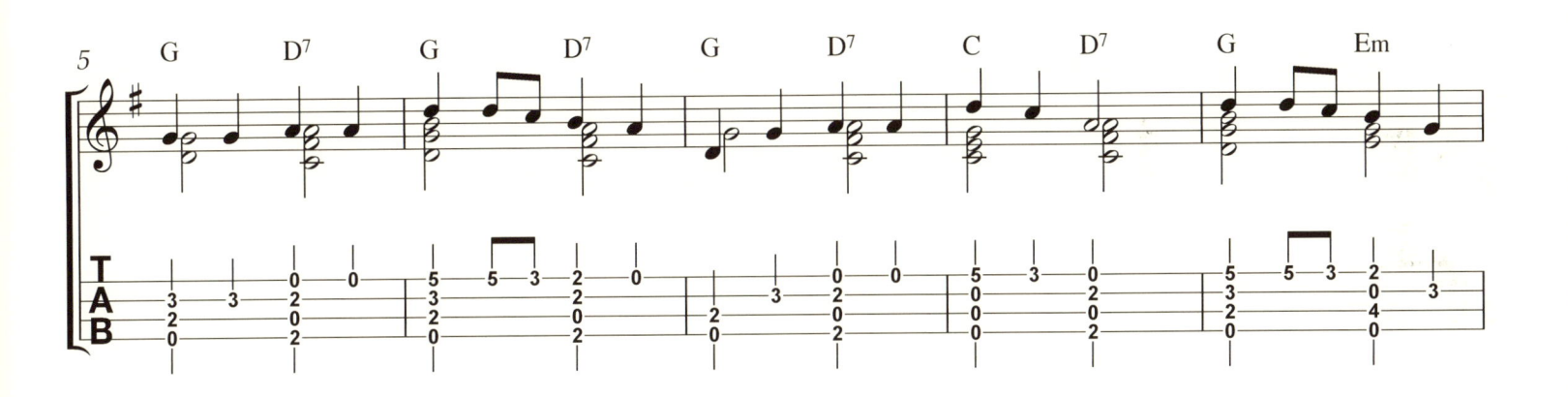

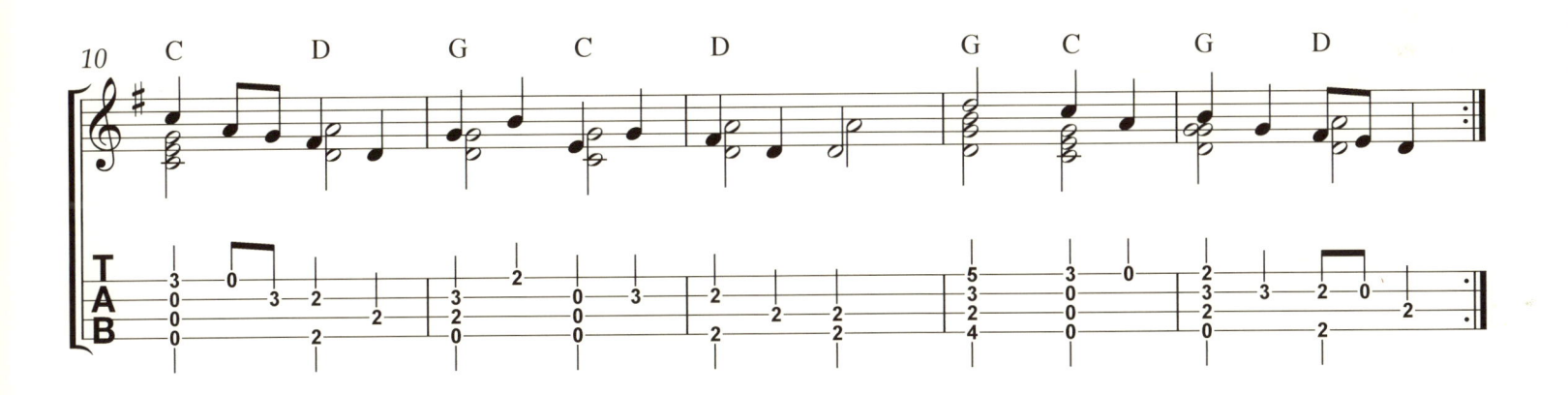

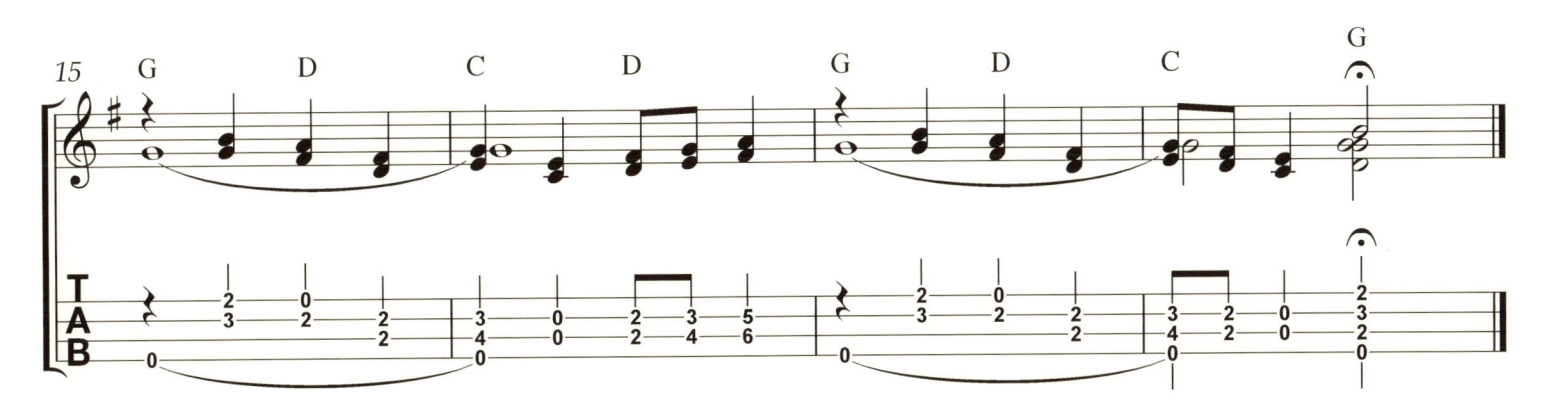

Track 19

19. Over the Hills and Far Away

Trad. arr. Colin Tribe

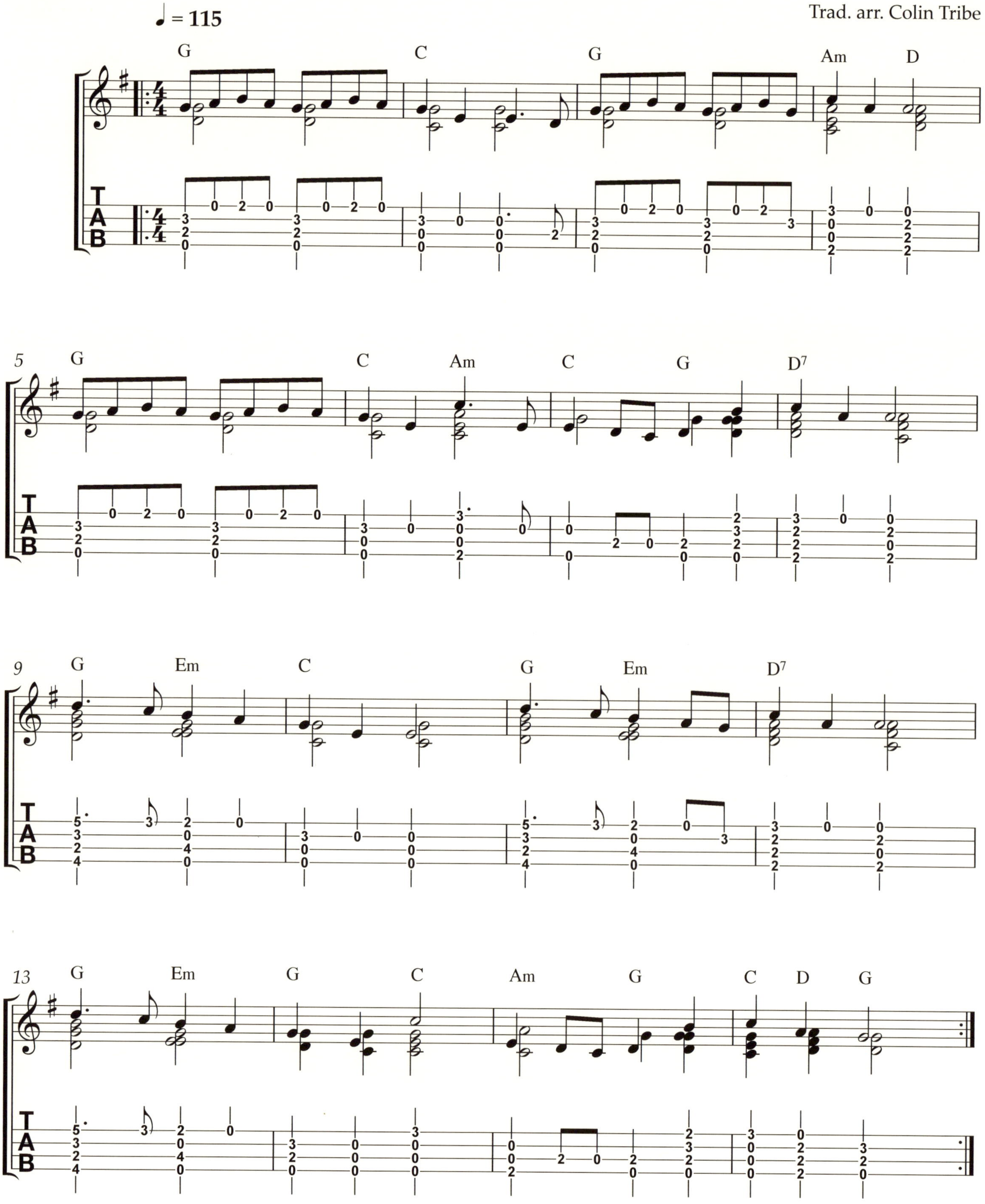

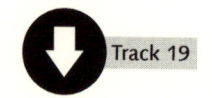

20. Raggle Taggle Gypsy

Trad. arr. Colin Tribe

♩ = 120 This can be played with a gentle swing

21. Sam Hall

Trad. arr. Colin Tribe

22. When the Boat Comes In
(Dance to Your Daddy)

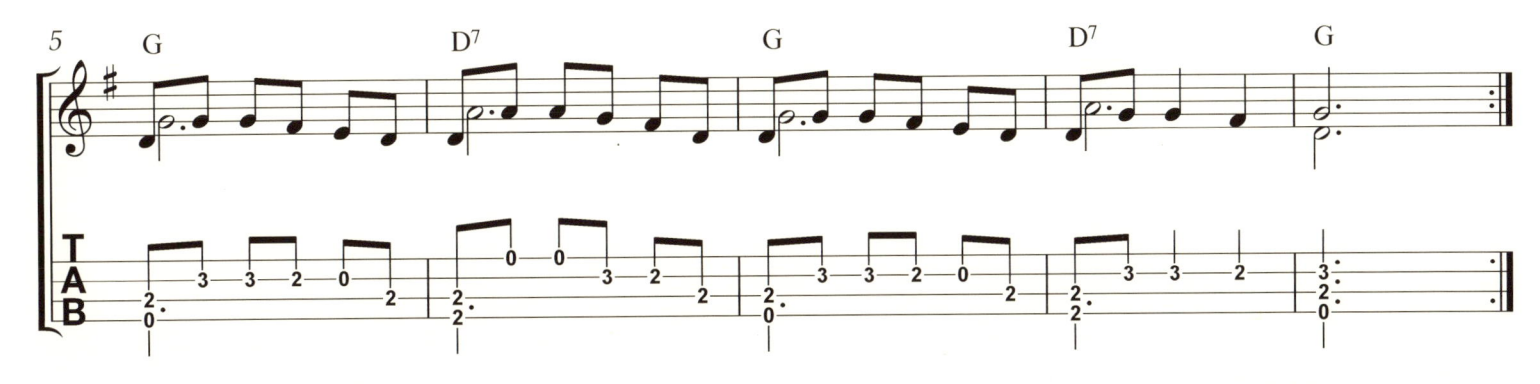

Trad. arr. Colin Tribe

23. Scarborough Fair

Trad. arr. Colin Tribe

29
Dm
C
Dm
Dm(add2)
34
F
Dm
G
Dm
Dm(add2)
39
Dm
F
44
C
Dm
C
Am
49
Dm
Dm(add2)
Dm

24. Spanish Ladies

Trad. arr. Colin Tribe

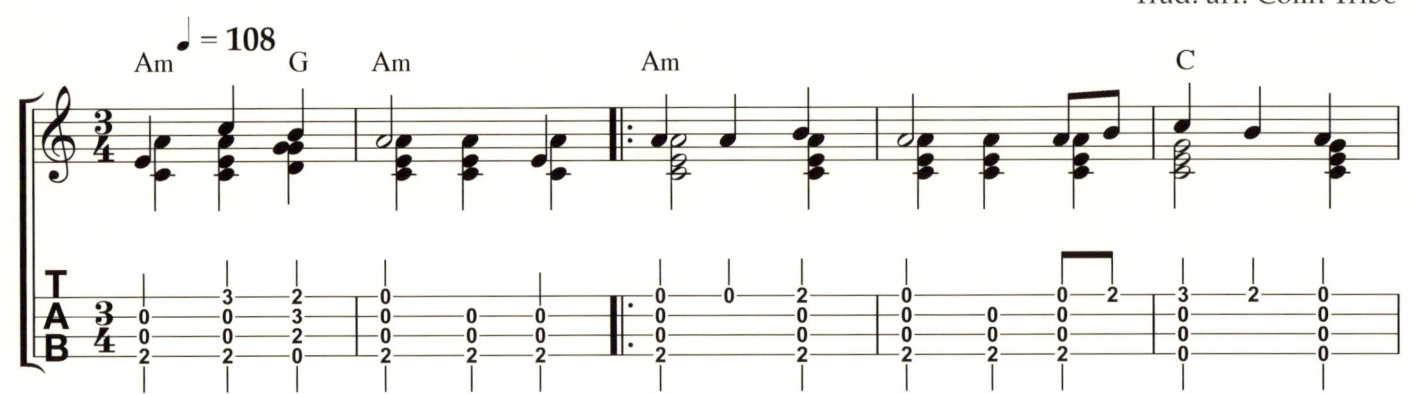

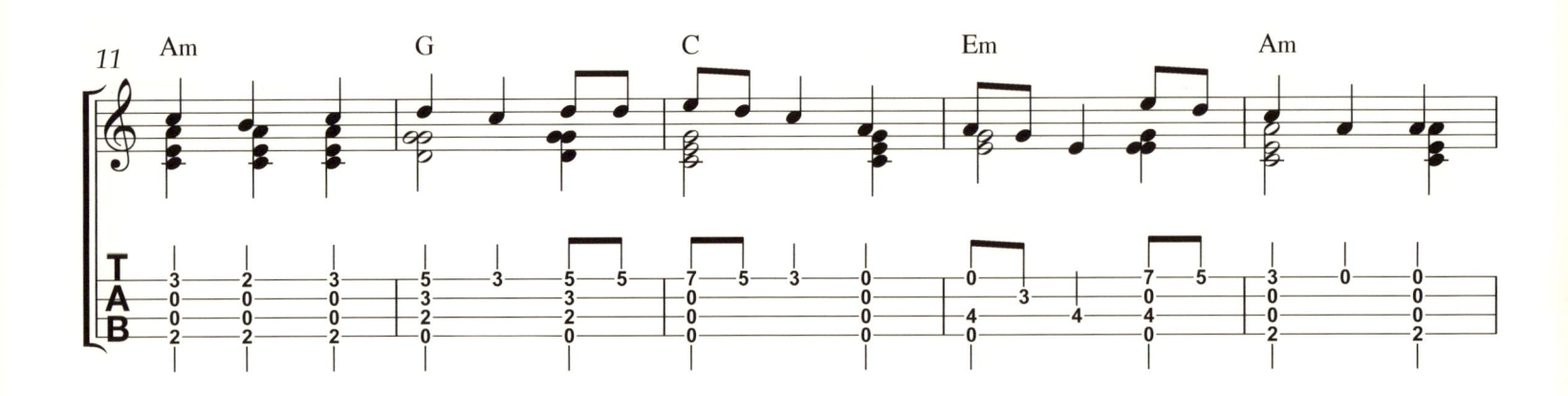

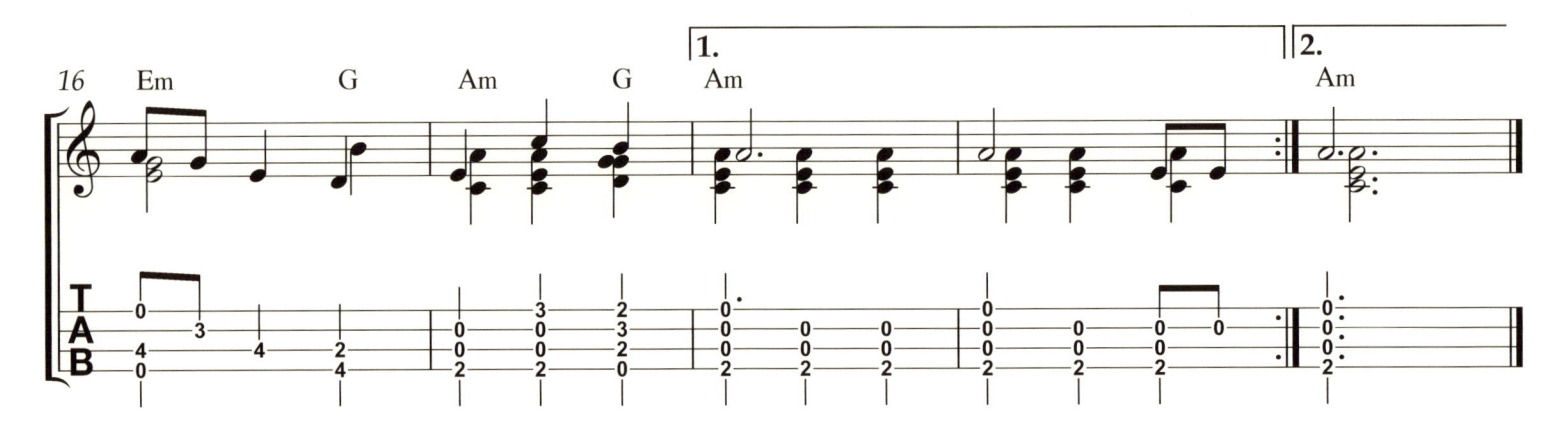

25. Stewball

Trad. arr. Colin Tribe

26. The British Grenadiers

Trad. arr. Colin Tribe

27. The Foggy Foggy Dew

Trad. arr. Colin Tribe

28. The Girl I Left Behind Me

Trad. arr. Colin Tribe

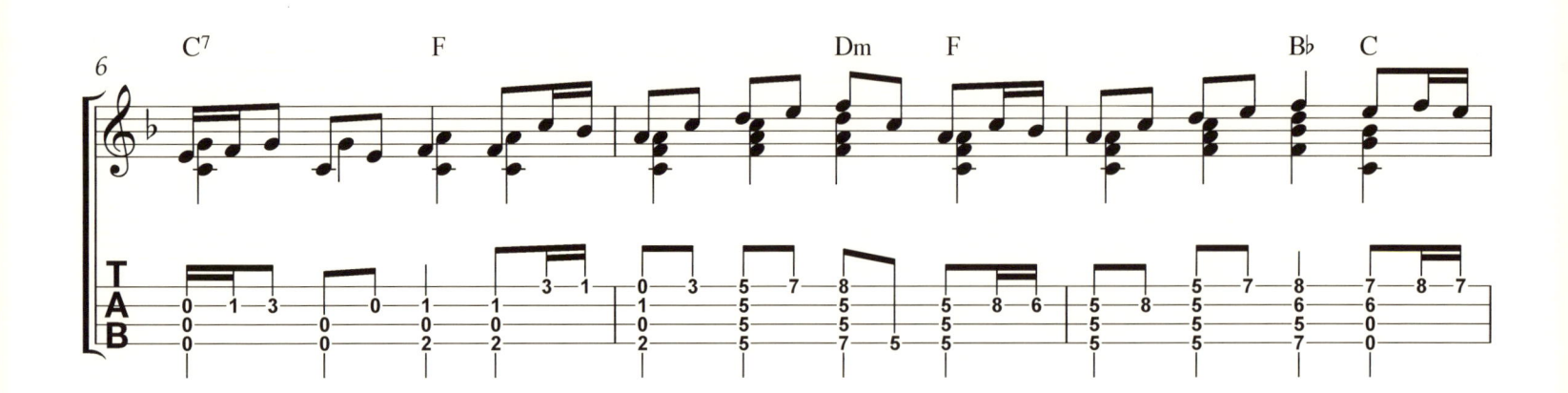

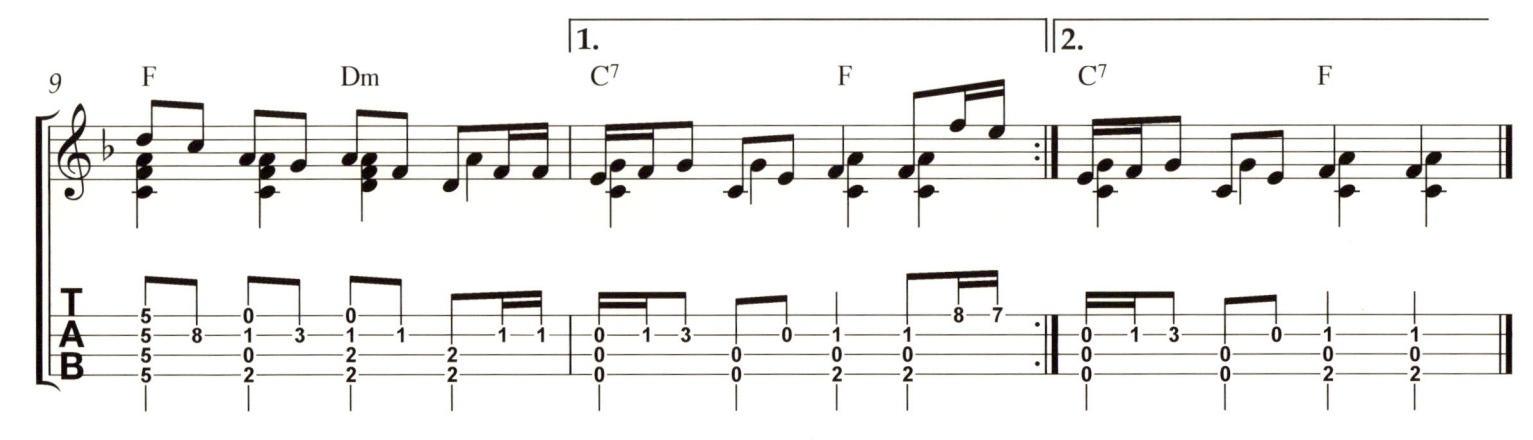

29. The Lass of Richmond Hill

Trad. arr. Colin Tribe

© 2013 Schott Music Ltd, London

30. The Keel Row

Trad. arr. Colin Tribe

31a. The Sailor's Hornpipe
(In F)

Trad. arr. Colin Tribe

31b. The Sailor's Hornpipe
(In G)

Trad. arr. Colin Tribe

32. The Water is Wide
(O Waly Waly)

Track 33

♩ = 60

Trad. arr. Colin Tribe

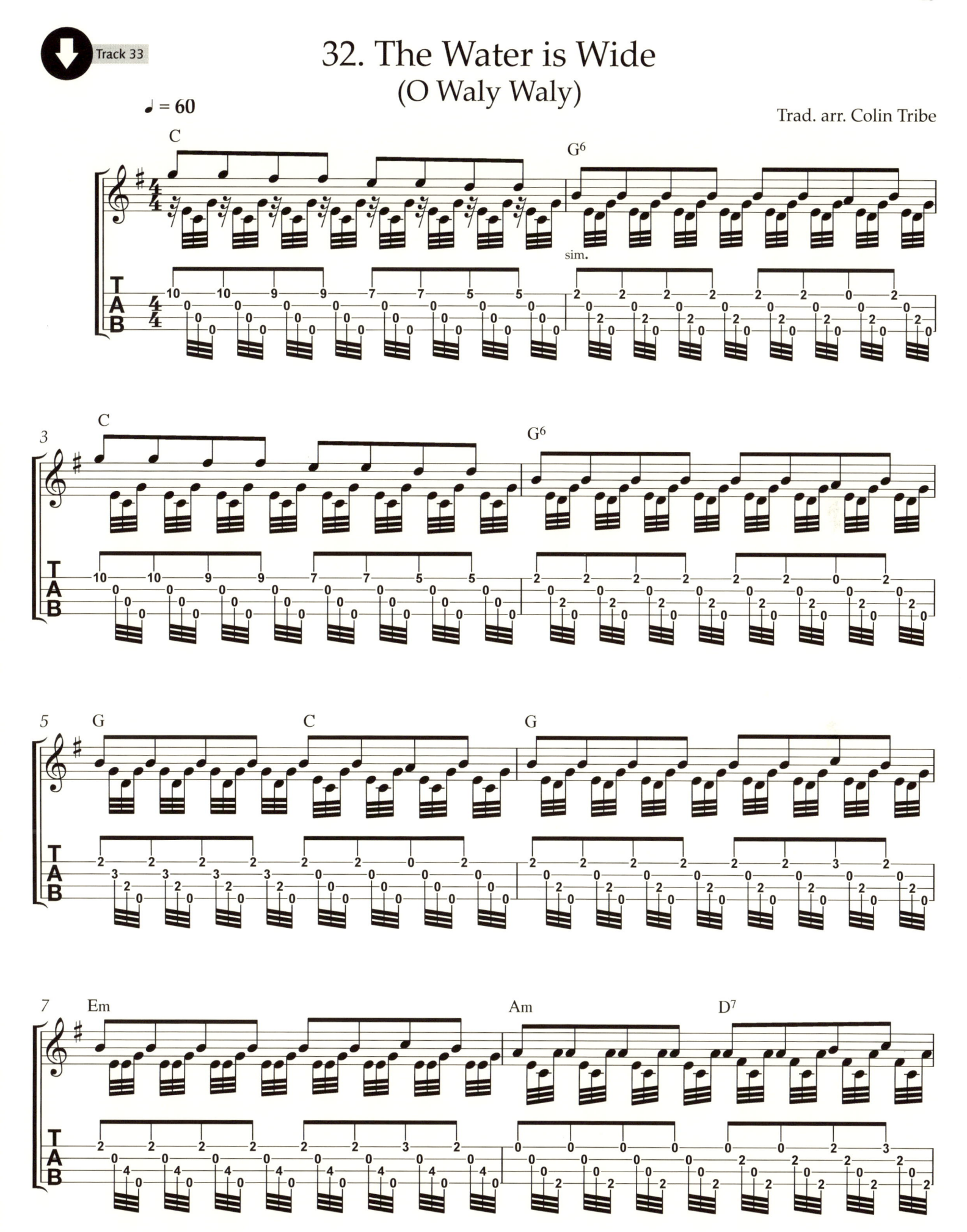

© 2013 Schott Music Ltd, London

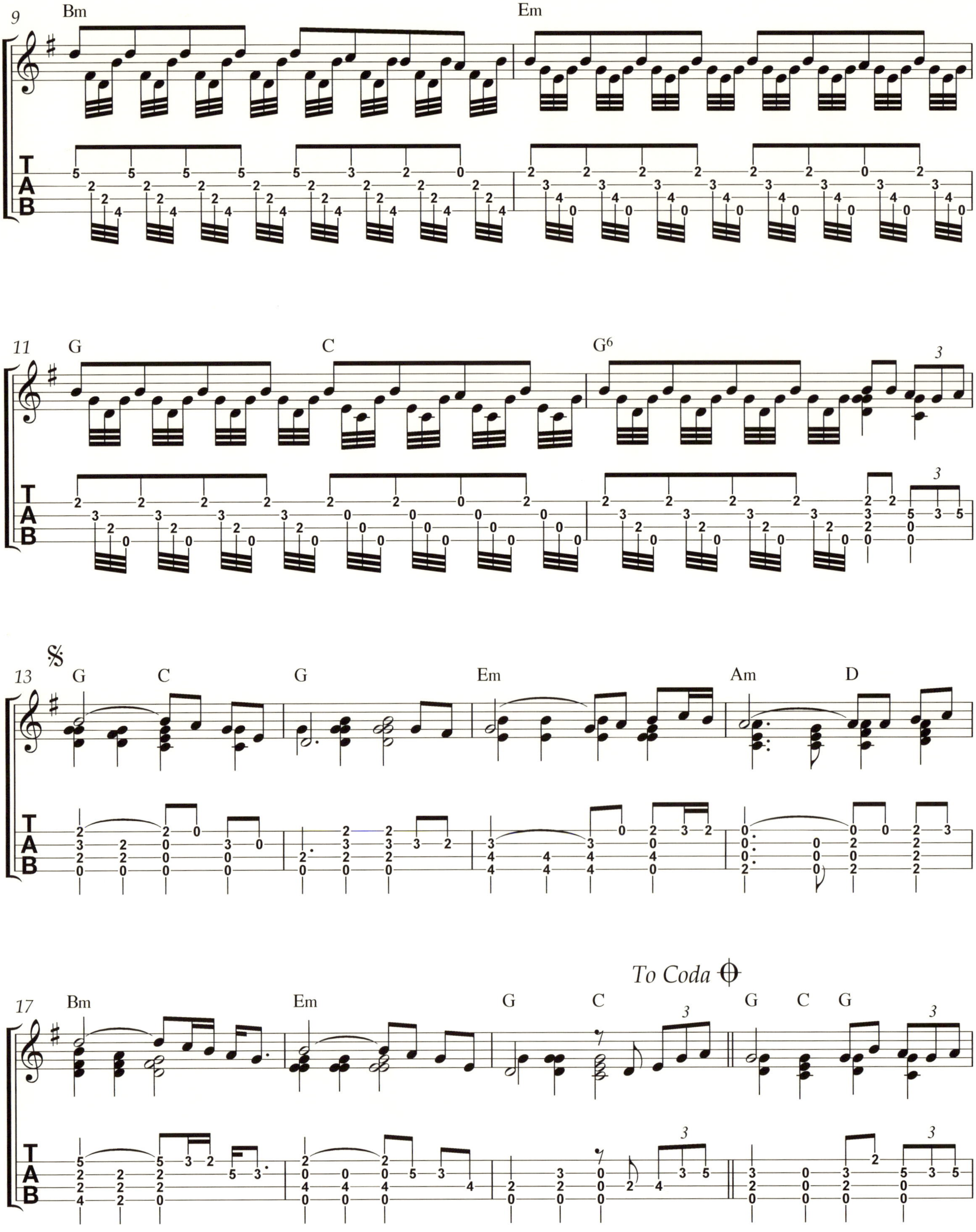
9
Bm
Em
11
G
C
G6
13
G
C
G
Em
Am
D
To Coda
17
Bm
Em
G
C
G
C
G

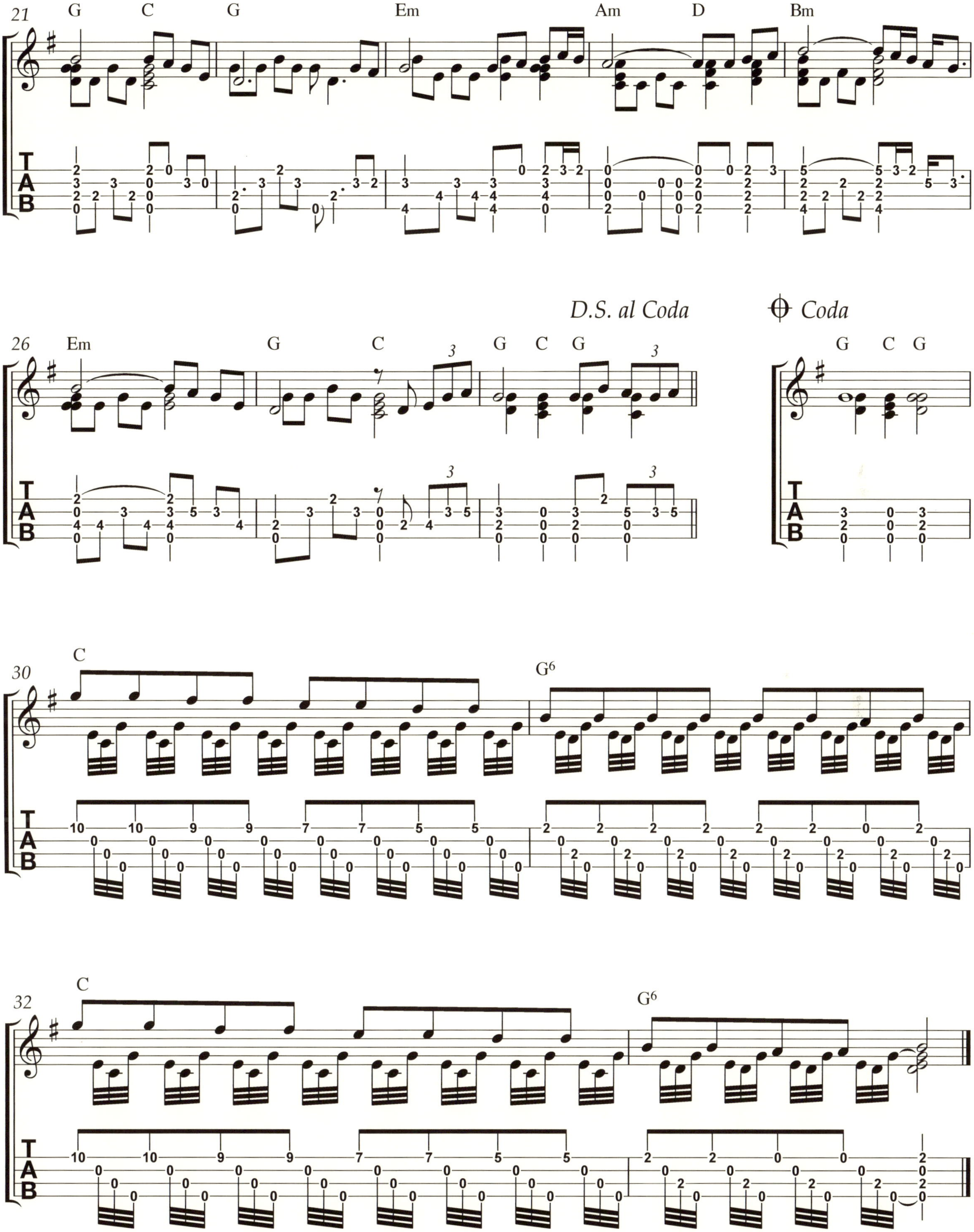
21
G C G Em Am D Bm
26
Em G C G C G
D.S. al Coda
Coda
G C G
30
C G6
32
C G6

33. The Lincolnshire Poacher

Trad. arr. Colin Tribe

© 2013 Schott Music Ltd, London

34. We Wish You a Merry Christmas

Trad. arr. Colin Tribe

35. The Ploughboy

Trad. arr. Colin Tribe

49

36. A Young Sailor Cut Down in His Prime

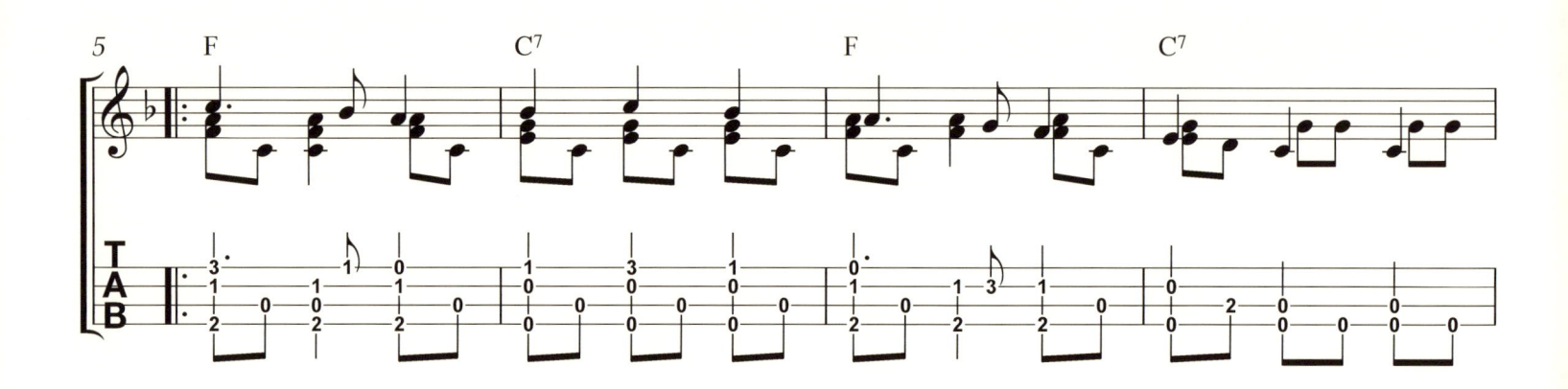

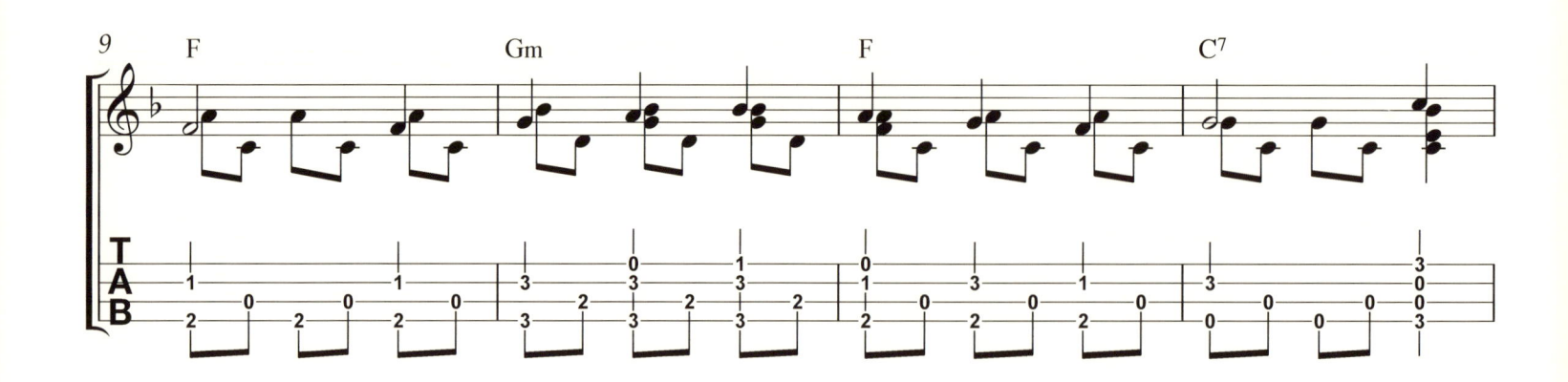

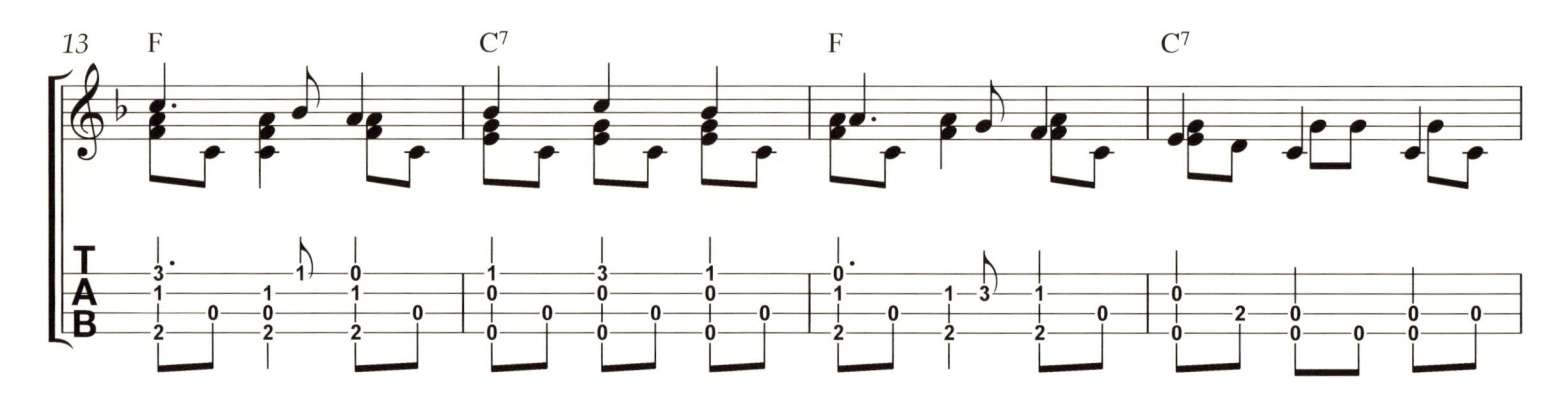

Trad. arr. Colin Tribe

17
F
Gm
F
C7
1.
F
C
2.
F
D7
TAB
21
G
D7
G
D7
TAB
25
G
Am
26
G
D7
TAB
29
G
D7
G
D7
TAB

52

37. What Shall We Do With the Drunken Sailor?

Trad. arr. Colin Tribe

Notes on the Tunes

1. As I walked Forth

As I walked forth one summer's day,
To view the meadows green and gay
A pleasant bower I espied
Standing fast by the river side,
And in't a maiden I heard cry:
Alas! alas! there's none e'er loved as I.

This song was written by Robert Johnson, a Jacobean lutenist and composer. He is most famous for producing original settings of lyrics for Shakespeare's later plays, working with the King's Men between 1610 and 1617. These are the only compositions known to have been written for the first performances of the plays.

This one shows a common feature of pieces in A (major or minor) in that it needs all 12 frets to be used to reach the high A. The small distance between higher frets as in Bar 13 E minor **0,11,0,10** need a raised left wrist to get good finger tip contact. Short nails on the right hand are essential.

In bar 2 use **5457** if **2007** is too much of a stretch.

2. Amazing Grace

Amazing Grace, how sweet the sound,
That saved a wretch like me.
I once was lost but now am found,
Was blind, but now I see.

John Newton was a sailor and slave trader who later underwent a spiritual conversion. Ultimately he became an Anglican clergyman and a vehement opponent of slavery. *Amazing Grace* was written as an hymn to illustrate a sermon he gave on New Year's Day 1773, while curate of Olney in Buckinghamshire. It was not until 1835 that the words were joined to the tune now almost invariably used, *New Britain*, in the American hymnbook *Southern Harmony*.

For technical notes, see page 6.

3. Blaydon Races

Aw went to Blaydon Races, 'twas on the ninth of Joon,
Eiteen hundred an' sixty-two, on a summer's efternoon;
Aw tyuk the 'bus frae Balmbra's, an' she wis heavy laden,
Away we went alang Collingwood Street, that's on the road to Blaydon.

George 'Geordie' Ridley, one of the most popular concert performers in Victorian Tyneside, wrote this song, first performing it in 1862. The tune was not Ridley's, but was lifted from an American song *On the Road to Brighton*. Suitably adapted, the song has been used as a chant by a number of football clubs, including Manchester United.

Note the B♭ - 4^3 in Bar 4 to give the C^7 chord. The G^7 in bar 7 can be fingered 1, 2, 3 or 2, 3, 4. In bar 24 try the repeated B♭ with *a,m,i, a,m,i* but include *pim* with the *a* on the chords.

4. Botany Bay

Farewell to old England the beautiful!
Farewell to my old pals as well!
Farewell to the famous Old Baily
Where I used to cut such a swell.

The destination for the first convict shipments to Australia in the 1780s, Botany Bay in New South Wales, inspired this Victorian song concerning the deportees' plight. It was performed at the Gaiety Theatre in London as part of *Little Jack Sheppard* in 1885. The music for this number is reputedly a traditional melody arranged by the theatre's musical director, Meyer Lutz.

Start with finger 2 in bar 1 and in bar 4 a pull of from 3^4 to 3^2 is a nice possibility. The F **2015** is a bit of a stretch but try it, the alternative could be **X555** with fingers 234 to allow Finger 1 for 1^3. The 1^5 to 1^3 in bar 7 could be pulled off as can 2^3 to 2^0 in bar 12. Bar 15 could have a hammer-on

From bar 17 a strumming pattern is introduced. Just use a gentle up and down *i* for this and don't worry too much about highlighting the tune until you get confident with it, the rhythmic element is more important. Eventually learn to pluck some of the melody notes on the first beat of each bar. Also don't fuss about hammers and pulls in that section.

5. Blow the Wind Southerly

Blow the wind southerly, southerly, southerly,
Blow the wind south o'er the bonny blue sea;
Blow the wind southerly, southerly, southerly,
Blow bonny breeze my lover to me.

The words of this Northumbrian folk tune were first published in 1834, but the melody is probably older. It was immortalised by Kathleen Ferrier in her 1949 recording of the song.

Again, fingering D **2220** gives rise to some alternatives. I like 312 in bar 3 as it allows the first finger to slide from fret 1 to 2 and back again to the A chord on either side. It is also good preparation for the F minor in bar 21. Bar 7 however needs a barre version.

In bar 10 slide with finger 4 from 1^4 to 1^7 and also try it in bar 11 although it is more difficult. Try to achieve a legato effect as you move from one chord to the next.

The second section from bar 26 uses a Pedal note A on the G string, use finger 2 for it. From bar 34 lots of fingering choices are possible, though I would avoid slides here. Bars 42 to 49 use a nice interplay between the 1st and 4th string in an alternating pattern using *a* and *p*

6. Early One Morning

Early one morning,
Just as the sun was rising,
I heard a young maid sing,
In the valley below.

The origins of this folksong are unclear. When William Chappell first published the tune in the 1850s he stated that he had heard it sung by workers from Yorkshire, Hereford, and Devon, showing how widespread the song had already become. It has been widely used in film and TV productions.

This is a slightly tricky piece that explores the A chord and its inversions fully. Perhaps spend time just changing from **2100** to **2104** to **6457** to **9,9,9,12** and back again, to get to know that pattern from Bar 7.

The opening bar uses a fingering 21 on both the first and second beats, a slightly unusual deployment of the 2nd finger which then moves back to fret 2 for the F♯ minor on the 3rd beat.

Use fingers 1,2,4 on the E^7 chord bar 2 leaving finger 3 for 1^2. The same shape as in bar 4, just a different order of notes.

After the sequence of A chords with the arpeggio ascending in bar 7 comes the scale of A descending, very satisfying.

From bar 9 the right hand needs to work hard, like a swan moving through water the body of sound needs to glide effortlessly whilst the legs are actually moving rapidly. Fortunately it is a very regular pattern that just needs repetition to get smooth. Note the repeated E notes against the descending scale in Bars 15 & 16; try to get it to stand out clearly.

7. Blow the Man Down

Come all ye young fellows that follow the sea,
to my way haye, blow the man down,
And pray pay attention and listen to me,
Give me some time to blow the man down.

A sea shanty, this may have originated amongst sailors working on transatlantic steamships, as the lyrics make reference to the Black Ball Line; this company ran ships from Liverpool to New York throughout the 19th century. Though the words were first published in full in 1879, the song gained widespread popularity through its inclusion in Laura Alexandrine Smith's anthology *The Music of the Waters* (London, 1888)

In bar 3 use a barre finger 1 for the D chord and finger 3 for the E note 3^4. D **2220** is an awkward chord and has many fingering variants (over 80 if you include the Thumb!) In bar 5 you could try the fingering **1120** with the 1st finger double stopping the G and C strings and this make it easier for the open A to sound clearly. Use 342 on the E minor shape for bar 11 as it leaves the first finger free for 2^2.

8. Dashing Away With the Smoothing Iron

'Twas on a Monday morning
When I beheld my darling,
She looked so neat and charming
In ev'ry high degree.
She looked so neat and nimble, O,
A-washing of her linen, O,
Dashing away with the smoothing iron,
She stole my heart away.

This song is part of a tradition of folksongs based around the days of the week, the action evolving chronologically through the verses. Cecil Sharp collected this folksong from a Captain Lewis at Minehead, Somerset in 1909.

Take notice of the harmonies provided on the 4th string. The re-entrant tuning of the instrument is one of its endearing qualities once you stop being frustrated and annoyed by it! I think it works for me because the Octave higher than expected 4th string is often played with the fleshy part of the thumb and is therefore softer than the other nail & pad plucked strings and so blends in effectively.

Of course in bar 8 the B♭ 4^3 melody note on the final quaver should be given an extra forceful twang to give it its melodic value. The preceding chord is a frequently used shape and worth studying. Note the **2124** F♯ minor in "Blow the Wind Southerly" is just the same shape shifted a fret down.

In the 2nd time ending bar, use finger 2 on 1^3 to allow the 3rd and 4th fingers to play 1^5 and 1^7.

9. English Country Garden

How many kinds of sweet flowers grow
In an English country garden?
We'll tell you now of some that we know
Those we miss you'll surely pardon

Before the First World War, Cecil Sharp collected a number of Morris Dance tunes which he arranged for solo piano. One of these, *Country Garden*, a handkerchief dance, was arranged in 1918 by Percy Grainger and dedicated to Edvard Grieg. The orchestral version of this led to its widespread use in schools and a status as a quintessential example of English folk music.

This is a fairly straightforward arrangement in C major. Hold fingers down as long as possible in the chord shapes to create a legato effect.

In bar 3 try to slide 2^2 to 2^3 as you play the C chord to highlight the melody note G.

In bar 9 use finger 2 for 1^3 and 4 for 1^5 and finger 4 for the 2^3 in the G^7.

For the A minor in bar 11 use finger 1 and 3 and then finger 2 moves from 1^2 to 2^2 with a bit of a stretch for finger 4 in the **2025** D^7 chord

10. God Rest Ye Merry Gentlemen

God rest you merry, gentlemen,
Let nothing you dismay,
For Jesus Christ, our Saviour,
Was born upon this day
To save us all from Satan's power
When we were gone astray.

O tidings of comfort and joy,
comfort and joy;
O tidings of comfort and joy!

This Christmas carol has a London origin and was first seen in print in the late 1700s. Evidently popular in the Victorian period, it is mentioned as being sung in Charles Dickens' *A Christmas Carol* (1843).

I love The Modern Jazz Quartet's version of this which John Lewis re-titled *England Carol Number 1*. It features some glorious improvised parts and can be found on YouTube. My version could perhaps be a basis for you to experiment on. The D minor **2215** is perhaps the only tricky chord. A double stop with finger 1 on G and C strings is the neatest solution to getting the fourth finger to reach the top note.

11. Greensleeves

Alas, my love, you do me wrong,
To cast me off discourteously.
For I have loved you well and long,
Delighting in your company.

This tune is traditionally attributed to King Henry VIII (d. 1547), though it first appeared in print in the 1580s. Nonetheless, it quickly gained popularity and was referred to in Shakespeare's *The Merry Wives of Windsor*. From that time it has endured in the various forms of folksong, hymn, and incidental music. As Michael Flanders expressed it, 'in every period play you go to see, whether it be set in 1300 up to about 1715 I suppose, still for incidental music, Greensleeves is always played'.

Play 1^3 in Bar 1 with finger 4 and the 1^6 with finger 2 which still holds 2^6 as it bends that joint to press on the first string. However for Bar 6 where the triplet figure follows, play the 1^6 with the tip of the finger after releasing it from 2^6.

In bar 3 you can use a Barre at the 3rd fret followed by 3^6 rather than 2^2 for the F# and the move the Barre to 2nd fret with lift to avoid first string for **2230**.

In Bar 10 the 4^7 allows you to keep the **7768** G minor chord in place.

12. Heart of Oak

Come, cheer up, my lads, 'tis to glory we steer,
To add something more to this wonderful year;
To honour we call you, as freemen not slaves,
For who are so free as the sons of the waves?

This song originated in the later 18th century, with music by William Boyce and lyrics by David Garrick, commemorating the year 1759 and its succession of victories for Britain in the Seven Years' War. The tune is now the official march of the Royal Navy.

Play the initial 4^0 G upbeat with the thumb, applying some force before the following *pima* roll chord. The melody note of this chord, on the top string, should sound slightly after the other notes to make it stand out.

Finger the G^7 in Bar 4 1,3,2 adding finger 4 on 1^7 for the E before lifting to allow the D to sound.

Bar 7 opens with **0987** - an Am^7 chord (although the accompanying part plays an A minor) to give a slight harmonic lift and also because it is a typical Ukulele motif! If you don't like it an alternative would be **5457** followed by 1^5 and 4^5.

13. I Gave My Love a Cherry

I gave my love a cherry without a stone
I gave my love a chicken without a bone
I gave my love a ring that had no end
I gave my love a baby with no crying.

This is a 15th Century English tune also titled *The Riddle Song*. A riddle is a puzzle and in this song the opening verse gives four statements that appear impossible. The second verse asks how they can be and the third verse gives an explanation. Such poetic licence, however, adds to the mystery of it all.

It has also been adapted for the pop song *The 12th of Never*, a big hit for Johnny Mathis where a bridge section was added to the original melody.

One neat way of highlighting the G, 2^3 at the start of Bar 6 is to slide up to it from 2^1 in the F chord. Slides can also be used effectively for the G7 chord in Bar 7 and from 1^{10} to 1^{12} in bars 8 and 12, but you don't have to use them each time.

14. Johnny Todd

Johnny Todd he took a notion
For to cross the ocean wide.
There he left his true love a-weeping
Waiting by the Liverpool tide.

Recorded in Frank Kidson's *Traditional Tunes* (1891), this folksong originated as a children's skipping song in the streets of Liverpool. However, versions of the song with different words were also found in Scotland and Ireland. The tune later inspired the theme to the BBC television series *Z-Cars* and was subsequently adopted by fans of Everton FC.

Play the opening with a hammer on from 2^0 to 2^1.

The B♭ **3215** in Bars 4 and 14 can be replaced with **7565**

The 2^3 in Bars 10 and 20 is best played with finger 4 so as to allow the 1^3 with finger 3 to keep ringing.

15. Married to a Mermaid

There was a gay young farmer,
Who liv'd on Salisbury plain;
He lov'd a rich Knight's daughter dear!
And she lov'd him again.
The Knight he was distressed,
That they should sweethearts be.
So he had the farmer soon pressed,
And sent him off to sea.
Singing Rule Britannia,
Britannia rules the waves
Britons never, never, never shall be slaves.

The idea that the music to this song was written by Thomas Arne (composer of *Rule Britannia*) in the 1740s is apocryphal. While this song shares a chorus with *Rule Britannia* (tune and lyrics), the respective words and music do not scan with each other. The present version achieved popularity through the music-hall singer Arthur Lloyd in the 1860s, though it could well have existed earlier as a seamen's song.

Play the 1^3 and 1^5 in Bar 3 with finger 4 sliding up from one to the other.

Play the *Rule Britannia* part from Bar 10 majestically!

Bar 15 Anchor the first finger on 2^1, Use 3 on 2^3 and 4 on 1^3

16. Morning has Broken

Morning has broken
Like the first morning
Blackbird has spoken
Like the first bird
Praise for the singing
Praise for the morning
Praise for them springing
Fresh from the word.

In the 19th century Mary Macdonald wrote a gaelic hymn, later translated as *Child in the Manger*. When the tune was first published it was named *Bunessan* after the village on the island of Mull where she lived. It is uncertain whether the tune was a traditional folk melody or whether it was devised by Macdonald. The song achieved particular popularity with schoolchildren after Percy Dearmer commissioned Eleanor Farjeon to write a new text – *Morning is Broken* for the hymn book *Songs of Praise*.

This may be the easiest piece in the book, but that simplicity calls for each verse to be treated with slight differences in the way the right hand plays the accompanying figures whist still keeping exactly the same left hand fingering. Try the pattern described for *Amazing Grace* and experiment!

I like the fingering 221 for the E minor **443X** in Bar 8.

In Bar 10 anchor the second finger on 3^2 and play the G shape in 11 as follows $3^2 = 2$, $2^3 = 4$, $1^2 = 4$, the G7 in Bar 11 is easily found by removing the 4th finger and using 1 on 2^1

You can find a more complex version on my Youtube channel (**http://www.youtube.com /user/colinrtribe**), which includes the famous piano introduction (originally played by Rick Wakeman) from Cat Steven's version of the tune.

17. Newcastle

Come you not from Newcastle?
Come you not there away?
O met you not my true love
Riding on a bonny bay?

The tune appeared in print as early as 1651 in John Playford's *The English Dancing Master*, a collection of country dances, but is thought to have its origins in the Elizabethan period. The song was included in Henry Fielding's play *The Grub Street Opera* (1731), though this was never publicly produced.

A song selected by my daughter Tania and one showing her confidence and prowess as a singer of lovely leaping melodies. For a soprano this key is also fine with a compass of E to high G and on the ukulele the open string C chord, $4^0 3^0 2^0$ is used quite extensively as in bars 11 and 13 with melody notes added on the A string.

Finger the G in Bar 1 with a barre on the top three strings and 2nd finger on 2^3 to make the 1^5 easier for the 4th finger to reach.

Except for the 1^7 in Bar 6 which is played with 4, use the first finger on all other 7th fret notes.

18. O No, John

On yonder hill there stands a maiden
Who she is I do not know;
I shall court her, for her beauty,
She must answer yes or no.

A Somerset folksong, a version was collected by Cecil Sharp and published in 1908. The tune appeared (with different lyrics, as *The Dumb Lady*), in the late 17th century.

For a light slightly whimsical touch to go with the lyrics of this song add pull-offs, hammers and slides to the introduction.

The D^7 **2020** is known as a 'Hawaiian D^7' and is an oddity in that it doesn't actually have a D in it! As I wanted the open A as the melody note I couldn't use the **2223** version of D^7 that is a more accurate sound.

In Bar 6 play 1^3 with the 3rd finger which then moves to the 2nd fret as the top note in the **2022** chord.

19. Over the Hills and Far Away

Our 'prentice Tom may now refuse
To wipe his scoundrel Master's Shoes,
For now he's free to sing and play
Over the Hills and far away.
Over the Hills and O'er the Main,

To Flanders, Portugal and Spain,
The queen commands and we'll obey
Over the Hills and far away.

The words and tune of this song appeared in print in 1709 as part of *Wit and Mirth, or Pills to Purge Melancholy*. Their origins are unknown. Since then the lyrics have varied significantly and the song has been turned to different emergent uses: as an Army recruitment song in the reign of Queen Anne, and later an anti-Jacobite one at the time of Bonnie Prince Charlie's revolt (1745).

The G **4235** in bar 9 is a very full sounding chord with the B added on the G string and one useful to use in accompanying as a variant to the open G version **0232**. Play the following melody note C 1^3 with the 2nd finger dropping on to it as a double stop on the top two strings. The E minor **0402** in the same bar is a useful variant from the more frequently seen **0432** or **4432** and makes the melody flow more easily.

20. Raggle Taggle Gypsy

Three old gypsies
came to our house door
they came brave and bawdy, oh
the one sang high and the other sang low
and the other sang a raggle taggle gypsy, oh.

This song is the product of a long oral tradition, beginning as a Scottish border ballad but spreading throughout the English-speaking world. It has gone by a number of names and has become best known to generations of children as *The Wraggle Taggle Gypsies O!* after its inclusion in Cecil Sharp's *English Folk Songs for Schools* (1906).

The fingering in bar 5 is the most complex part of this fairly easy arrangement. A barre at the 2nd fret for the D chord **2220**, with a lift of the first finger to let the melody note A sound prominently, is a good solution. The first finger then drops down to the 2nd fret to complete the barre for **2222** and stays there for the B minor chord **4225**. Fingers 234 can then be used on the E minor.

From bar 10 the right hand goes into overdrive, using *i* to play the C string notes on all the off-beat quavers.

21. Sam Hall

Oh me name it is Sam Hall chimney sweep, chimney sweep
Oh me name it is Sam Hall chimney sweep
Oh me name it is Sam Hall and I've robbed both great and small
And my neck will pay for all when I die, when I die
And my neck will pay for all when I die

Jack Hall was a notorious thief who was convicted of burglary at the Old Bailey and hanged in 1707. In his youth he had been a chimney sweep, as the lyrics of the folksong relate. The precise origins of the song are unknown, but from the mid-19th century versions begin to refer to *Sam Hall* and this name has become the generally accepted variant.

A song played on many gigs by the Newark Ukulele Band in Nottingham, and one that has a very American blues feel to it in spite of its English heritage. The use of both B♮ and B♭ in the melody gives this impression. This flavour can be found in the slide from bar 13 to 14, the presence of C^7 chords and the **2021** to give a D7♭9 chord. Having these features makes it a natural piece in which to try some improvised choruses using blues scales, bending notes etc.

22. When the Boat Comes In

Dance to your Daddy, my little laddie
Dance to your Daddy, my little man
Dance to your Daddy, sing to your mommy
Dance to your Daddy, my little man.

This has been variously described as a sea shanty, folk song, and nursery rhyme. It has clear connections with Northumbria. The words now used are attributed to William Watson in *The Tyne Songster* (1840); it was to be sung to the tune *The Little Fishy*, which may have been an existing Tyneside song.

Play the opening G with a 3 string barre and then lift the first finger to play the open A or use fingers 132 and have a larger stretch out with 4 for 1^5. It would also be possible to substitute 2^5 for 1^0 and 3^4 for 2^0 if you wish. Rob Tribe did the recording using his right hand thumb, and it could also work with a plectrum.

23. Scarborough Fair

Are you going to Scarborough Fair?
Parsley, sage, rosemary, and thyme;
Remember me to one who lives there,
She was once a true love of mine.

The fair at Scarborough was an important one in medieval Yorkshire, attracting merchants from across Europe and reputedly lasting 45 days each summer. It has been suggested the song originated from this period and area.

I have used ideas from *Simon and Garfunkel*'s superb version to give the Dmi^2 chord and the harmony in Bar 44. It is a modal piece so I have not put in a D minor key signature! The reach to **2215** D minor is tough but worth working on as an alternative. **2555** does not give as many different notes and makes the moves to surrounding melody notes more difficult.

24. Spanish Ladies

Farewell and adieu to you, Spanish Ladies,
Farewell and adieu to you, ladies of Spain;
For we've received orders for to sail for old England,
But we hope in a short time to see you again.

The song was used in the Royal Navy, first mentioned in the ship's log of the *Nellie* in 1796. While its precise origins are unknown, it is widely thought that it grew out of the Napoleonic Wars when British forces were in contact with Spain.

The abundance of open strings in this demands careful left hand and wrist positioning to give the strings maximum ringing freedom. Basically, raise the wrist to give a high arch to the hand.

An interesting fingering idea comes in bars 6 and 11. They start with the same notes but because of the next part of the melody, play bar 6 with finger 2 on 2^3 & 3 on 3^4 and bar 7 with 1 on 2^3 and 2 on 3^4 so that fingers 3 and 4 are free for the 1^5 and 1^7.

25. Stewball

Oh Stewball was a racehorse
And I wish he were mine
He never drank water
He always drank wine.

The English racehorse Stewball (or Skewball) achieved fame for his phenomenal 1752 season in Ireland, where he won six races worth £508. Although the song was already circulating in the 18th century, it achieved significant popularity in the southern USA from the mid-1800s, widely used as a chant by chain gangs. The place names in the song were there substituted for American ones.

Another one in which I have borrowed ideas from a famous modern versions of the melody – it was re-used by John Lennon in *Happy Christmas (War is Over)* where he skilfully placed it in three different keys and I have used the G sus^2 harmony from that. I also remember listening to the *Peter, Paul & Mary* version when that first came out with its delightful close harmonies that find echoes here. The strumming element in this, to keep the rhythm of the first bar, is important to give the horse racing feel full reign.

26. The British Grenadiers

Some talk of Alexander, and some of Hercules
Of Hector and Lysander, and such great names as these.
But of all the world's great heroes, there's none that can compare.
With a tow, row, row, row, row, row, to the British Grenadiers.

Based on a tune dating from the 17th century, this song was first used as a march by the Grenadier Guards in 1706. The words probably date back to the War of the Spanish Succession (1702-1713). The march is used by a number of regiments in Britain and Canada, and is played annually at the ceremony of Trooping the Colour.

A variation in the opening bar is quite instructive. I suggest you use a *pim* roll on **201X** then include the open C. If, however, in a repeat you use a pinched chord to start with then missing out the open C is fine as it is played as the melody note immediately afterwards.

For the rapid semiquavers start each time by using an alternating *m,i* pattern.

27. The Foggy Foggy Dew

When I was a bachelor, I liv'd all alone
I worked at the weaver's trade
And the only, only thing that I ever did wrong
Was to woo a fair young maid.
I wooed her in the wintertime
And in the summer, too
And the only, only thing that I did that was wrong
Was to keep her from the foggy, foggy dew.

By the time Cecil Sharp collected this folksong it was found throughout Britain, though its origins are thought to lay in East Anglia. It was first published in 1815.

Bar 1 shows a way around the lack of available notes on the ukulele. It starts with the D chord on beat 1 (DF♯A) and then changes to D^7 (CF♯A) on beat 3 after the D has been established and won't be missed!

Bar 14 has a subtle move on the G string to include the B on the 3rd beat when it is replaced by the melody D note 1^5.

In the final bar I have put in a 4^2 to give the effect of a perfect cadence (D to G); just shift the 1st finger over to achieve it.

28. The Girl I Left Behind Me

The hours sad I left a maid
A lingering farewell taking
Whose sighs and tears my steps delayed
I thought her heart was breaking
In hurried words her name I blest
I breathed the vows that bind me
And to my heart in anguish pressed
The girl I left behind me

In the 1840s this was considered to be one of the most popular folksongs in Britain, played whenever a naval ship weighed anchor or a regiment left the town in which it was quartered. It appeared in print in the 1790s but probably has a much longer pedigree as a folk tune.

The tablature of this shows some solutions to the problem of keeping the harmony in the most accessible places to facilitate the melody. However, feel free to find alternatives, using the chart on page 5 and of course through your own experimentation.

The joy of using a software programme like Sibelius is that alternatives can be found by just dragging the notes around. A case in point is the C melody note in bar 3. The most obvious position for it is 1^3 but that does not make it easy to harmonise the D note preceding it so I have used 2^8 with a 5th fret bar as again in bar 7.

Practice moving from F in 1st position **2013** to F at the 5th, **5558** to make this become fluent.

29. The Lass of Richmond Hill

*On Richmond Hill there lives a lass
More bright than May-day morn,
Whose charms all others maids' surpass,
A rose without a thorn.*

Often mistaken for a genuine folksong, this number was a collaboration between the barrister and lyricist Leonard McNally and the composer James Hook; it was first performed in 1798 and was a favourite of King George III. Despite having a club foot and walking with a limp, Hook enjoyed a highly successful career as a concert organist at the fashionable pleasure gardens at Pentonville, Marylebone, and Vauxhall.

Use a 1st finger 4th fret Barre to give an E chord from Bar 12. In Bar 11 however, use finger 3 for the Barre to allow it to stay in place for the B chord that follows.

There is quite demanding use of rapid finger 4 movements to play the melody notes 2^4 and 1^5 in Bar 6.

30. The Keel Row

*As I came thro' Sandgate,
Thro' Sandgate, thro' Sandgate,
As I came thro' Sandgate,
I heard a lassie sing.*

Another Tyneside folksong connected with maritime Newcastle, it appeared in print in 1770 though is probably much older. In spite of its close Northumbrian connections, some have suspected the tune has Scottish origins due to the presence of 'Scotch Snaps' in the rhythm.

The presence of some rhythmic twists and melodic leaps make this a fun one to play. Try to not be lazy and perform it as a swing time piece, the dotted quavers should last for $3/4$ of a beat not $2/3$.

Use a hammer-on with finger 4 in bars 9 and 13 to go from 1^5 to 1^{10}; it will need some effort to get it to work clearly but it sounds good after the preceding Scotch Snap rhythm (♫)!

31. The Sailors Hornpipe

The *College Hornpipe* was first published in 1798, based on sailors' dances performed onboard ship. Quoted in innumerable musical arrangements and used in a variety of films and TV programmes, the hornpipe has achieved particular immortality as part of Sir Henry Wood's *Fantasia on British Sea Songs*, invariably played at the Last Night of the Proms.

I have done two versions of this. The one in F is playable on a 12 fret instrument whilst the G version needs 14 frets but puts it in the same key as the version in Schott Music's recent publication *English Folk Tunes for Guitar* (ED 13491) by Hugh Burns.

Pull-offs and hammer-ons are essential to the flow of the tune and following the tablature will help you get the correct fingering to make it work. There is a video of the G version on my Youtube channel (**http://www.youtube.com/user/colinrtribe**).

Try to make the section from bar 11 sound like arpeggios with the notes ringing on in *Campanella* style.

32. The Water is Wide

*The water is wide, I cannot cross o'er.
And neither have I the wings to fly.
Build me a boat that can carry two,
And both shall row, my true love and I.*

Cecil Sharp collected this song and published it in *Folk Songs from Somerset* (1906), but there seem to be influences from both England and Scotland in the words and the music. There were formerly a wide variety of lyrics, but Sharp's version – consolidating several sources – has come to be the accepted one.

Here in a slightly more involved arrangement, my intro represents the lapping of the water – meandering down the G major scale from a C chord before introducing an impressionistic version of the melody from bar 4. The full melody starts at the end of Bar 12 and eventually wistfully returns to the rippling water motif for the ending.

Obviously the backwards ***pima*** stroke, ***a,m,i,p*** will need to be mastered for the opening, but until it has been you could start at the end of Bar 12.

Attempt as much legato effect as possible; pull-offs in 13, 17 & 18, and a hammer-on or slide in 19.

In the arpeggiated version, from bar 21, I have stopped the arpeggios at those same places to allow the melody a little more freedom.

33. The Lincolnshire Poacher

*When I was bound apprentice in famous Lincolnshire
Full well I served my master for nigh on seven years
Till I took up to poaching as you shall quickly hear
Oh, 'tis my delight on a shiny night in the season of the year.
Oh, 'tis my delight on a shiny night, the season of the year.*

This is a traditional Lincolnshire folksong, first appearing in print around 1775. It became the march of the Royal Lincolnshire Regiment and is also used by RAF College Cranwell.

Hold the E^7 **1202** with fingers 1, 2 & 3 and then add the fourth finger for the G♯, 2^4 in bar 3.

In bar 8 you can use 1^4 instead of 4^6 for the C♯.

34. We Wish You a Merry Christmas

*We wish you a Merry Christmas
and a Happy New Year.
Glad tidings we bring to you and your kin;
Glad Tidings for Christmas and a Happy New Year.*

This carol has its origins in the West Country in the 16th century. The lyrics refer to the tradition of bands of carollers visiting the houses of the wealthy, receiving food and drink as payment – hence the promise that the singers would not leave until they had got their 'figgy pudding'.

There is a lovely chord progression round part of the circle of fifths in this fairly straightforward short tune. The B^7 is the only tricky fingering issue; making sure you have enough space for the 3rd finger to play 1^3. Slightly angle the 1st finger to make room for this.

35. The Ploughboy

A flaxen-headed cowboy, as simple as may be,
And next a merry plough boy, I whistled o'er the lea;
But now a saucy footman, I strut in worsted lace,
And soon I'll be a butler, and whey my jolly face.

Though often treated as a traditional folksong this piece was written for the 1787 opera *The Farmer*, with music by William Shields and lyrics by John O'Keefe. Benjamin Britten reinterpreted it in his collection of *Folksong Arrangements* for voice and piano (Volume 3, 1947)

Another piece in A and by now, if you are working through the book alphabetically, you will have got used to the chord shapes that occur in this key. A new one might be the B^7 in bar 16 and again from 26, **4656**.

In Bar 34, aim for a legato approach, hammering on the 1^7 and 1^4.

36. A Young Sailor Cut Down in His Prime

One day as I strolled down by the Royal Albion
Cold was the morning and wet was the day
When who did I meet but one of my shipmates
Wrapped up in flannel yet colder than clay.

The Unfortunate Rake is a traditional folk ballad first written down in 1790. Various versions have been sung in which young soldiers, sailors or maids are "cut down in their prime" and contemplate their deaths. An American version, *The Cowboy's Lament* also known as *The Streets of Laredo*, is now the most well known set of words to the tunes.

This is another long time favourite melody of mine, although I was more used to the *Streets of Laredo* version until I heard this in the background to a funeral in a recent BBC TV series *Ripper Street*. I have provided variation by using three different keys and my hope is that this will make you familiar with the different harmony ideas that can crop up in those tonalities, providing some inspiration for when arranging pieces for yourself.

Notice the three different forms of accompaniment used and how transposing is achieved by the use of the Dominant 7th chord each time.

Verse 1, in F, has a repeated dominant note C – easy to play in this key because of the open C string.

Verse 2, in G, has an accompanying chord on each beat.

Verse 3, in A, has one chord per bar except for two needed for the perfect cadence in bar 52.

37. What Shall We Do with the Drunken Sailor?

What shall do with the drunken sailor,
What shall do with the drunken sailor,
What shall do with the drunken sailor,
Ear-ly in the morning?

A sea shanty coming out of America, it was first described in 1839 being used by whalers in Connecticut. It was in the early 20th century that it gained widespread popularity on both sides of the Atlantic and was included in a much-used collection of shanties edited by RR Terry (*The Shanty Book*, 1921). The tune was utilised by other composers, including Malcolm Arnold, Percy Grainger, and Fritz Spiegl (in the 'UK Theme' for BBC Radio 4).

Another piece in the Dorian mode like *Scarborough Fair* and highly suitable for the Ukulele because of its lowest note of C. Notice how it is made up of chord notes and scale passages throughout.

I use an F harmony in bars 9 and 17 because I like it and it fits with my basic notion of having as much harmonic movement in Ukulele arrangements as feasible to add variety to the limited resources at hand.

Use either a ***pima*** roll or a pinched stroke on the chords to give another aspect of variety.

About the author

Colin Tribe is a self-taught musician born in 1946 who grew up as a teenager with the sounds of skiffle, jazz, American rock and The Beatles explosion. The guitar was his second instrument (after recorder in Primary School - his only formal lessons) and by the age of 17 he had music published for guitar by BMG and a song writing contract. The projected career as a musician was overtaken by a love of teaching, but not initially of music as, after college, he began a career as a Primary School teacher combing this with a flourishing life as a semi-professional guitarist and singer in various bands.

Eventually his love of music became an academic focus when he completed a performing arts degree before starting to teach music. Whilst Head of Music at Highbury Grove in London he was invited to present the electronic keyboard syllabus he had developed to a working party at Trinity College of Music leading to his arrangements and compositions being used in their first electronic keyboard exams. When Victoria College of Music (VCM) wanted to extend the range of exam material to include diploma level they asked if he would be interested in contributing, and so more advanced pieces were arranged and a long and very happy relationship with VCM was established.

In the meantime his musical life had also taken in 'cello, bassoon and mandolin with arrangements of Bollywood film music becoming a passion. Along with Jane Morgan in the band *Wild Thyme* his song writing found new life in a mix of styles including folk, jazz and poetry – whilst school life was always a driving force to explore new genres of music that would appeal to his students in Islington.

The VCM syllabus for guitar was his next major work as he retired from full time teaching and began work as an examiner. Then, whilst developing a syllabus for Self-Accompanied Singing (which includes a set of books for Ukulele players), an addiction to the ukulele began and he was able to create an exam for players who wanted to develop melodic fingerstyle skills in addition to those of the standard strumming accompaniments. This is now published, up to Diploma Level and there are teachers and students taking the exams in the UK & Ireland and as far away as Malaysia, Toronto, San Francisco, Taiwan and Australia.

Colin considers himself primarily a composer and arranger although also loves performing, especially for his Youtube channel and in the informal settings created by ukulele groups worldwide.

Some comments on Colin's recent work:

"Lovely arrangements!" - *Jim Beloff*

"Your arrangements are truly wonderful!" - *Liu Tsun Tsien*

" A gifted arranger, able to take the essence of a song and translate it to the limited musical palette of the ukulele, using melodic highlighting, harmonic suggestion, and rhythmic articulation" - *Michael Kenfield*

"The way you play it, it sounds like it was written for the uke" - *James Likos*

VCM Grade Listings

One piece at each grade can be chosen as an alternative selection for those wishing to take the Victoria College of Music Ukulele Exams.

A
Melody only versions of -
Morning has broken, What Shall We Do with the Drunken Sailor, When the Boat Comes In

B
Full versions of -
Morning has broken, What Shall We Do with the Drunken Sailor, When the Boat Comes In

C
Botany Bay, God Rest Ye Merry Gentlemen,

D
O No John, We Wish You A Merry Christmas

1
Blow the Man Down, Over the Hills and Far Away, Spanish Ladies, The Foggy, Foggy Dew

2
Blaydon Races, Dashing away with the Smoothing Iron, English Country Garden,
Married to a Mermaid, Raggle-Taggle Gypsy, Stewball, Greensleeves,

3
Hearts of Oak, I Gave My Love a Cherry, Newcastle, Sam Hall,
The British Grenadiers, The Lincolnshire Poacher

4
As I walked Forth, Johnny Todd, Scarborough Fair, The Girl I left behind me,
The Lass of Richmond Hill, Young Sailor Cut Down in His Prime

5
Amazing Grace, The Keel Row, The Plough Boy, The Sailor's Hornpipe (F & G)

6
Blow the Wind Southerly

7
Early One Morning

8
The Water is Wide

Track List

1	As I Walked Forth	1:06
2	Amazing Grace	1:18
3	Blaydon Races	0:40
4	Botany Bay	0:56
5	Blow the Wind Southerly	1:47
6	Early One Morning	1:21
7	Blow the Man Down	0:44
8	Dashing Away with the Smoothing Iron	0:53
9	English Country Garden	1:11
10	God Rest Ye Merry Gentleman	0:52
11	Greensleeves	0:46
12	Heart of Oak	1:09
13	I Gave My Love a Cherry	2:02
14	Johnny Todd	0:48
15	Married to a Mermaid	1:24
16	Morning Has Broken	1:16
17	Newcastle	0:53
18	O No, John	0:55
19	Over the Hills and Far Away	0:58
20	Raggle Taggle Gypsy	1:00
21	Sam Hall	1:05
22	When the Boat Comes In	0:38
23	Scarborough Fair	1:17
24	Spanish Ladies	0:52
25	Stewball	0:51
26	The British Grenadiers	0:51
27	The Foggy Foggy Dew	1:00
28	The Girl I Left Behind Me	0:55
29	The Lass of Richmond Hill	1:13
30	The Keel Row	0:38
31	The Sailor's Hornpipe (In F)	1:12
32	The Sailor's Hornpipe (In G)	1:09
33	The Water is Wide	2:17
34	The Lincolnshire Poacher	0:51
35	We Wish You a Merry Christmas	1:03
36	The Ploughboy	0:59
37	A Young Sailor Cut Down in His Prime	1:49
38	What Shall We Do With the Drunken Sailor?	1:01

Total Duration   **41:40**